Mango and Peppercorns

Mango
and
Peppercorns

**A Memoir of Food,
an Unlikely Family, and
the American Dream**

By Tung Nguyen,
Katherine Manning,
and Lyn Nguyen
with Elisa Ung

Foreword by
Michelle Bernstein

CHRONICLE BOOKS
SAN FRANCISCO

Library of Congress Cataloging-in-Publication Data

Names: Nguyen, Tung (Restaurateur), author. | Manning, Katherine (Restaurateur), author. | Nguyen, Lyn, 1976- author. | Ung, Elisa, author. | Bernstein, Michelle, author of foreword.

Title: Mango and peppercorns / by Tung Nguyen, Katherine Manning, and Lyn Nguyen, with Elisa Ung ; foreword by Michelle Bernstein.

Description: San Francisco : Chronicle Books, 2021.

Identifiers: LCCN 2020031855 | ISBN 9781797202242 (hardcover) | ISBN 9781797202938 (ebook)

Subjects: LCSH: Nguyen, Tung (Restaurateur) | Manning, Katherine (Restaurateur) | Cooking, Vietnamese. | Restaurateurs--Biography.

Classification: LCC TX724.5.V5 N6 2021 | DDC 641.59597--dc23

LC record available at https://lccn.loc.gov/2020031855

Manufactured in China.

MIX
Paper from
responsible sources
FSC
www.fsc.org
FSC™ C008047

Design by Vanessa Dina.
Typesetting by Frank Brayton.
Typeset in Albra Text and Applied Sans.

10 9 8 7 6 5 4 3 2 1

Chronicle Books LLC
680 Second Street
San Francisco, California 94107
www.chroniclebooks.com

To all the immigrants and refugees who
are working toward a better opportunity for
themselves and their families

Foreword

M
A
N
G
O

A
N
D

P
E
P
P
E
R
C
O
R
N
S

Long before I went to culinary school or won the James Beard Award for Best Chef: South, and long before I had even gone to high school, I had a dining experience that inspired my approach to food.

I was twelve years old, and the restaurant was Hy Vong, owned by Tung Nguyen and Kathy Manning, in my hometown of Miami. My teenage sister had just eaten there with her boss and said we absolutely *had* to go. Our meal was full of these deep umami flavors that reached from our tongues to our souls. An hour after we finished, we headed back to the restaurant for more spring rolls.

From that day on, nothing satisfied me like the food of Hy Vong. It was a tiny hole in the wall. You had to write your name with a pencil on a list. You had to wait forever to get a seat, and then wait forever to give your order, and then wait forever for your food. But it didn't matter. It was so good, and so fun, and everyone who was anyone was eating at Hy Vong: celebrities; chefs; people of every age, race, and sexual orientation. And they were all constantly *talking* to each other—in ways I have seen in few other restaurants—asking other customers whether they had tried the special, or speculating exactly how Tung fried the shallots.

Tung remained my cooking role model long after my first experience with her food. She had an authenticity that I have strived for my entire career. As I cooked in other kitchens and trained as a chef, even after I opened restaurants of my own, I returned to Hy Vong as often as I could. I tried to sneak peeks at Tung in the kitchen, studying her ingredients and techniques. I admired how she never compromised for American palates by using excess sugar—which is pretty amazing given that most of her customers were not Vietnamese. I credit Hy Vong for teaching generations of Miami residents about Vietnamese food and culture.

There is nothing like Hy Vong. I craved its food like no other—so much that I even had Tung and Kathy cater my wedding. I'm thrilled that they have finally put some of their famous recipes into a book. I've been begging for their recipes for years!

Yet even more than their food, I am inspired by their story. We never know whom we are going to end up with in life. What are the odds that these women—unlikely friends, raised on different continents, who didn't always get along well when they finally did meet—ended up with such magic between the two of them? I can't tell you what it is, but I wish I had a piece of that magic.

It's such an American story: A pregnant, hardworking Vietnamese refugee meets a strong midwestern woman with a big personality. Together they open a cherished, widely acclaimed restaurant, creating their success as a business owned entirely by women—all while raising a child.

They got more than they expected. We all did.

Michelle Bernstein

LATE CITY EDITION
Weather: Turning cloudy today; cool tonight. Partly sunny tomorrow. Temperature range: today 46-65; Wednesday 42-54. Details, Page 81.

"All the News That's Fit to Print"

The New York Times

VOL. CXXIV...No. 42,831

© 1975 The New York Times Company

NEW YORK, THURSDAY, MAY 1, 1975

Price higher in air delivery cities.

20 CENTS

Ford Delays Oil Fee Rise, But Will End Price Curbs

President Again Prods Congress to Act on Energy—Democrats Expected to Fight 2-Year Phase-Out of Controls

By EDWARD COWAN
Special to The New York Times

WASHINGTON, April 30—President. The Administration is another prod to Congress to plan, as outlined at a White enact comprehensive energy House news briefing by Frank legislation, the White House G. Zarb, Federal Energy Adminannounced today that Presi-istrator, is to reduce the volume dent Ford was again deferring of price-controlled crude oil by an increase in the special fee about 4 per cent a month for on imported crude oil but that two years. Presumably, the he was starting an administra-present average ceiling price on tive process that could end all oil still under controls would price controls on domestic crude remain unchanged at $5.25 a oil in two years.

The move to phase out the remaining controls on crude oil prices was expected to provoke new frictions between the Republican President and some Democrats in Congress.

However, the White House left open the possibility that Mr. Ford might sign legislation that would extend the domestic period to three and a half or four years, if Congress were to pass such a provision into an energy bill otherwise acceptable to the

Continued on Page 29, Column 1

Amtrak, at Age of 4, Still Problem-Ridden

By RALPH BLUMENTHAL

Amtrak executives and a Federal judge riding the Metroliner from Washington to New York recently for a hearing including train delays, inadequately became prime exhibits when they got stuck behind a slow-moving freight train and pulled in 35 minutes late.

A week later, some of the same Amtrak officials taking the Broadway Limited to Chicago for another of the hearings arrived an hour and a half late after a burning coal from the kitchen stove set the dining car afire before the train even left Penn Station.

As it marks its fourth birthday today, Amtrak, the country's semiconsolidated rail passenger system, remains plagued by embarrassing mishaps and breakdowns that have embroiled it in controversy with the Interstate Commerce Commission over the quality of its service.

Over the last two months, scores of disgruntled Amtrak riders have appeared at I.C.C. hearings around the country to complain about a wide range of problems from broken air-conditioning to vermin infestation to early train personnel.

Continued on Page 44, Column 2

FARMERS' PRICES UP 4%, IMPLYING RETAIL RISE SOON

Cattle and Hogs Are Among Main Items That Climbed in Month Ended April 15

By WILLIAM ROBBINS
Special to The New York Times

WASHINGTON, April 30—Prices of farm commodities rose 4 per cent in the month ended April 15, the Agriculture Department reported today. A top departmental economist noted that the increase was focused largely in areas where it would be most quickly reflected at the retail counter.

Increased prices for cattle and hogs were among the main reasons for the rising average. Cotton, soybeans and grains also gained.

"Price changes for cattle and hogs come through to the consumer pretty fast," Kyle Randall, administrator of the Agriculture Department's economic research service, said, but he added that the rise had been expected.

The increase reversed a five-month slide in farmers' prices. The April 15 level was still 6.1 per cent below the average of last October, before the decline began, and 7 per cent below the level of a year ago.

Outlook Unchanged

Mr. Randall said the farm-price rise would not change Agriculture Department economists' assessment of the outlook for food prices.

"Our original forecast was for an increase in livestock prices in the second quarter," he said. "but we are standing by our prediction that retail prices from the first to the second quarter won't rise as much as they did from the fourth to the first quarter."

He said retail prices were expected to rise "something less than 3 per cent" in the second quarter. The increase in the first quarter was 3 per cent.

Coincidentally, the turn in farm prices comes at a time when President Ford is expected momentarily to veto a bill voting off the South Vietnamese vets.

Action in Congress

The long slide in farm prices had helped stimulate the movement in Congress for the farm bill, which would increase both "target prices" and price-support loans for cotton and grains and price supports for dairy products.

Target prices set off subsidy payments when market prices fall below the target level. The price-support loans enable farmers to withhold products when market prices are weak. House farm-bloc leaders had already described the prospects

Continued — Page 36, Column 7

COMMUNISTS TAKE OVER SAIGON; U.S. RESCUE FLEET IS PICKING UP VIETNAMESE WHO FLED IN BOATS

Graham A. Martin, center, the United States Ambassador to South Vietnam, being escorted aboard the U.S.S. Blue Ridge yesterday after his arrival by helicopter. Mr. Martin was one of the last persons to leave his embassy

Kissinger Says U.S. May Shelter 70,000

By JOHN W. FINNEY
Special to The New York Times

WASHINGTON, April 30—United States Navy ships continued today to pick up South Vietnamese refugees fleeing their country in small boats, the State and Defense Departments reported.

In addition to 6,000 South Vietnamese evacuated by helicopter yesterday from Saigon along with 1,373 Americans, the State Department, said, 22,000 South Vietnamese have been picked up by Navy ships waiting off the South Vietnamese coast.

As the flow of refugees continued, Secretary of State Kissinger, who yesterday used a figure of 50,000 refugees, estimated that the United States might have to resettle as many as 70,000 South Vietnamese.

Mr. Kissinger told reporters in Capitol Hill that the Administration would soon ask Congress for funds to handle the resettlement of the refugees.

Philip C. Habib, Assistant Secretary of State for East Asian and Pacific Affairs, estimated that as much as $500-million might be required over the next year to take care of the refugees.

The Defense Department declined to say how many ships had been left in position to pick up South Vietnamese who were able to flee by small boat into the South China Sea. As for the legal authority to continue the rescue effort now that Americans have been evacuated from South Vietnam, Joseph Laitin, Assistant Secretary of Defense for Public Affairs, said at a Pentagon briefing: "There is no law that says you can't pick up people in distress on the high seas."

The Defense Department declined today to say whether the ships were remaining in the international waters, outside the three-mile territorial limit claimed by the former South

Continued on Page 15, Column 2

Vietnamese Government. There is some question, however, whether this limit still applies, since North Vietnam, and presumably the Provisional Revolutionary Government, which is taking over control in Saigon, claim a 12-mile territorial limit.

Confusion over the territorial limit claimed by North Vietnam was a key element in the Gulf of Tonkin incident in August, 1964, which led to a Congressional resolution authorizing President Lyndon B. Johnson to introduce troops into South Vietnam. The Defense Department at first contended that two destroyers that it said had come under North Vietnamese attack were in international waters but later acknowledged that they had gone within the 12-mile limit claimed by North Vietnam.

SAIGON REDS LOOK TO NONALIGNMENT

Regime, in Paris Statement, Also Pledges to Protect Lives of Foreigners

By FLORA LEWIS
Special to The New York Times

PARIS, April 30—The war in Vietnam is over, the Provisional Revolutionary Government said here today in a statement hailing "a victory of historic significance for the South Vietnamese population."

The statement, which followed the surrender of Saigon to the Vietnamese Communist Text of statement in Paris is on Page 14.

early today, said the new South Vietnamese regime would follow a foreign policy of "peace and nonalignment," and gave assurances that the lives and property of foreigners in the country would be protected.

The statement was issued by Dinh Ba Thi, the head of the South Vietnamese Communist delegation here that was established under the 1973 Paris agreement to negotiate a political solution with the Government of President Nguyen Van Thieu.

"Henceforth," the statement said, "South Vietnam is free and independent, the sacred testament of our beloved President Ho Chi Minh is realized. No details were issued here

Continued on Page 14, Column 3

'HO CHI MINH CITY'

Communications Cut Soon After Raising of Victory Flag

By GEORGE ESPER
The Associated Press

SAIGON, South Vietnam, April 30—Communist troops of North Vietnam and the Provisional Revolutionary Government of South Vietnam poured into Saigon today as a century of Western influence came to an end.

Scores of North Vietnamese tanks, armored vehicles and camouflaged Chinese - built trucks rolled to the presidential palace.

The president of the former non-Communist Government of South Vietnam, Gen. Duong Van Minh, who had gone on radio and television to announce his administration's surrender, was taken to a microphone later by North Vietnamese soldiers for another announcement. He appealed to all Saigon troops to lay down their arms and was taken by the North Vietnamese soldiers to an undisclosed destination.

[Soon after, the Saigon radio fell silent, normal telephone and telegraph communications ceased and The Associated Press said its wire link to the capital was lost at 7:28 P.M. Wednesday, Saigon time (7 A.M. Wednesday, New York time).

[In Paris, representatives of the Provisional Revolutionary Government announced that Saigon had been renamed Ho Chi Minh City in honor of the late President of North Vietnam. Other representatives said in a broadcast monitored in Thailand that former Government forces in eight provinces south of the capital had not yet surrendered, but no fighting was mentioned.]

The transfer of power was symbolized by the raising of the flag of the National Liberation Front over the presidential palace at 12:15 P.M. today, about two hours after General Minh's surrender broadcast.

Hundreds in Saigon Cheer

Hundreds of Saigon residents cheered and applauded as North Vietnamese military vehicles moved to the palace grounds from which the war against the Communists had been directed by President Nguyen Van Thieu, who resigned April 21, and by President Ngo Dinh Diem, who was killed in a coup in 1963, in broadcasting today in the

Continued on Page 14, Column 1

A War History

An illustrated review of the long conflict in Vietnam appears on Pages 17 through 20.

Legislature Votes U.D.C. at $228-Million

By LINDA GREENHOUSE
Special to The New York Times

ALBANY, April 30—The Legislature voted tonight to give the Urban Development Corporation $88-million and to lend $140-million as the state's part of a delicate agreement with the major commercial banks to make it possible for the insolvent agency to repay its debts and finish its building programs.

Tonight's action, which the two houses took with obvious reluctance at the end of a day of partisan wrangling, was the price that the 11 clearing-house banks had set for their willingness to lend the U.D.C. $140-million. That loan is due to be

Continued on Page 44, Column 3

$104,000 Damages And Former Job Won By College Teacher

By WALTER H. WAGGONER
Special to The New York Times

FREEHOLD, N. J., April 30—A judge ordered today that Brookdale Community College reinstate a journalism professor who had criticized the college president, and that the college president and six trustees each pay her $10,000 in punitive damages.

The teacher, Patricia Endress, was awarded a total of $104,000 in damages and lawyers' fees.

"Punitive damages are absolutely necessary to impress people in authority that a employee's constitutional rights cannot be infringed," said Judge Merritt Lane in Superior Court here.

Last June 27, three days before Miss Endress would have gained tenure, the college's board of trustees voted to terminate

Continued on Page 26, Column 4

1975 MEETS 19TH CENTURY IN WALL STREET: Frank Malara, dressed as a town crier for re-enactment of Washington's inaugural at Federal Hall National memorial, preparing to announce the event as a young woman in 19th-century garb passed. A report, Page 45.

Marines carrying children who were restored when a copter carrying them from Vietnam crashed on deck of U.S.S. Blue Ridge, command ship, Tuesday. All were saved.

Thieu Aide Discloses Promises Of Force by Nixon to Back Pact

By BERNARD GWERTZMAN
Special to The New York Times

WASHINGTON, April 30—A State former Saigon Cabinet official made public today letters from President Richard M. Nixon that promised the Saigon Government in 1972 and 1973 that the United States would "take swift and severe retaliatory action" and would "respond with full force" if North Vietnam violated the Paris cease-fire accords.

This was believed the first disclosure of any such actual Texts of letters released by former minister, Page 18.

correspondence between Mr. Nixon and former President Nguyen Van Thieu of South Vietnam. The White House conceded earlier this month that there had been letters between the leaders as part of an exchange surrounding the signing of the 1973 cease-fire. An aide of Secretary of

Kissinger said at that time that in one letter before the signing, Mr. Nixon promised that the United States would react to a major Communist attack, but that specific.

The contents of the letters made public by Nguyen Tien Hung, former Minister of Planning, seemed more specific about the possible use of American retaliatory military force than the White House disclosure briefly earlier this month when the matter of secret assurances to Saigon first became an issue.

Coincidentally with Mr. Hung's disclosures, at a crowded news conference in the Mayflower Hotel, President Ford formally refused to give Con-

Continued on Page 16, Column 4

NEWS INDEX

Introduction

As the Vietnam War came to a close in the spring of 1975 with North Vietnam victorious, people began to flee impending Communist rule. Many escaped in boats, enduring days on the open ocean. Those who survived the journey were taken into refugee camps throughout Southeast Asia.

The United States, which had supported South Vietnam in the war, sponsored the evacuation of 125,000 Vietnamese refugees, who resettled throughout America. Tung Nguyen was one of the first to arrive. She had fled Saigon as the North Vietnamese Army approached the city. After a harrowing nine-day boat trip and a brief stay in Guam, she was transported to Fort Indiantown Gap in central Pennsylvania. The military base was one of four U.S. processing centers for Vietnamese refugees, taking in more than 20,000 people over a period of eight months.

After two months in the camp, Tung, who was twenty-seven at the time, was resettled in Miami by Lutheran World Relief. Katherine Manning, a thirty-year-old graduate student and cashier at the University of Miami, volunteered to temporarily host Tung and eleven other refugees until they found places to live.

Tung and Kathy went on to become two of Miami's most successful restaurateurs. This is their improbable story, along with recipes for some of their most popular dishes.

RECIPE NOTE: *The recipes in this book were tested using Morton kosher salt, Tung's preference. If you use a different type of salt, you may need to adjust the amount.*

Who's Who

Note: Some names have been changed to protect the privacy of individuals.

THE AUTHORS

Tung Nguyen: Born in 1948 in Vietnam, escaped Saigon in April 1975 and resettled in Miami later that year; called *Mẹ* (Vietnamese for *mother*, pronounced "Maa," with the "aa" sounding like the "a" in *apple*) by her daughter, Lyn

Lyn Nguyen: Tung's daughter, born Phuong Lien Nguyen in March 1976 in Miami; changed her name in her twenties

Katherine (Kathy) Manning: Born in December 1944 in Iowa, moved to Miami as a teenager; volunteered to host Tung and other Vietnamese refugees in 1975

VIETNAM AND THE REFUGEE CAMP

Bà Nội (grandma): Tung's paternal grandmother

Tung's mother and father

Mau, Kiem, Nhut, Lai, Thuong, and Hiem: Tung's six living younger siblings

Sinh: Tung's friend in Saigon

Ông and Bà Hoang: a couple from Hanoi whom Tung met at the refugee camp in Pennsylvania (*Ông* and *Bà* are honorific titles for a man and a woman, respectively, similar to *Mr.* and *Mrs.*)

Minh: a man whom Tung met at the refugee camp and to whom she was briefly engaged

KATHY'S FAMILY IN IOWA AND MIAMI

Grandma Peterson: Kathy's maternal grandmother

Gwendolyn Manning: Kathy's mother, who eventually moved in with Kathy, Tung, and Phuong Lien; called Grandma by Phuong Lien

FRIENDS AND OTHER REFUGEES

Thao: Kathy's college friend and roommate, originally from Đà Nẵng, Vietnam

Huong: Thao's brother, who escaped the fall of Đà Nẵng in late March 1975 and was the first refugee Kathy hosted

Luc and Tay: "cousins" of a big family of refugees who also lived with Kathy

TUNG'S PARTNERS IN MIAMI

Bao: Tung's first husband

Duc: Tung's partner after her divorce from Bao

OTHER VIETNAMESE IN MIAMI

Bà Hang: a woman who lived near Hy Vong and introduced Tung to both Bao and Duc

Bà Hien: a woman from Hanoi who owned an Asian grocery store

EMPLOYEES IN MIAMI

Carlos: a longtime busboy at Hy Vong and then at Tung Restaurant

Jay: one of Tung's first cooks, who began working for her in 1998

15

PROLOGUE

The Long Walk

Miami, 1981

TUNG:

Kathy didn't listen. Kathy never listened. And it was time to teach her a lesson, Vietnamese-style.

My arrival in Miami six years earlier was not easy. Everything seemed so much brighter and more jarring than I had known in Vietnam, and my ears hurt from how loudly Kathy yelled all of the time. Her house was filled with people who treated me poorly. All of it made me speak to my dead grandmother, wondering whether her spirit had guided me to the wrong place.

The not listening had gotten worse after we opened a restaurant together. She didn't listen when I told her to pay the electric bill. That became clear when the lights and air conditioning went out and our customers sat in a dark room, sweating. She didn't listen when I told her the water bill was due, even though it should have been obvious I couldn't make soup if no water came out of the faucet. She just kept talking to me in that loud voice that hurt my ears, like everything else in America.

But that same loud voice made my baby laugh and laugh, especially when little Phuong Lien—the reason I got up each day and fought for a place to belong in America—was riding around the house on Kathy's back. Kathy was also the only one who knew everything about how I got to this country. The only one who knew the terrible guilt I felt over leaving my family. She even knew how I had become pregnant, and she accepted me anyway. And each time I said "Trời có mắt" ("God has eyes"), she nodded and understood.

On the morning she called me from jail looking for a ride home, I decided not to help Kathy with her latest problem. I had more important things to do and did not want to fight about something that was her own fault. Hy Vong would be open for service in a few hours, and I had to make stock, cut several chickens for the popular curried chicken and sweet potatoes, fillet kingfish, thinly slice a bunch of lemongrass, and do a million other things. Our lives depended on my work. Kathy had to figure out things on her own, or she would never learn.

KATHY:

I spent most of my night in jail avoiding the toilet. The stench of urine filled the air in the tiny, windowless cell. As the hours passed, I began to dread having to pee in front of the two other women sitting on the wooden bench with me. Who knew you could land in jail for not getting your car inspected on time?

If it was going to happen to anyone, it was going to happen to me. It certainly wasn't my first time in jail for something stupid. *Kathy, you've done it again*, I told myself. I had a history of making bad decisions that landed me in trouble. Sometimes, opening a restaurant with Tung seemed like one of them.

Owning a restaurant meant there was always something that needed to be done right then and there. There was no time for routine errands, like renewing a car registration. From the minute I woke up to the time I left Hy Vong at 2 a.m., my life was dictated by the needs of the restaurant: going to the butcher to buy meat or to the market for ripe tomatoes; waiting on tables; making sure guests left full and happy; sweeping floors and cleaning the bathroom; dragging heavy garbage bags into the alley and hoisting them over my head into the dumpster.

After I forgot to pay the electric and water bills, I had to call the utility companies to beg them to reinstall our service as fast as possible. And when I failed to do one of the tasks on my never-ending list, I had to listen to Tung yelling from the kitchen.

But that yelling faded into the background every time I tasted Tung's food. The deep flavors of her cooking filled me with such joy. I also felt so much pride when our customers raved about their meals, and when restaurant critics wrote glowing reviews about Hy Vong. I wanted Tung to do what Tung did best: cook. I knew that meant I had to do everything else. But it was so much harder than I expected.

As night turned to morning in the jail cell, I kept shifting, trying to get comfortable on the hard bench. I hoped I could leave soon. I worried about Tung and Phuong Lien. Had they made it home safely after we got pulled over for an expired inspection sticker and I was escorted to the police car?

I heard footsteps outside the cell and suddenly the door swung open. "You can go," an officer said. I exhaled deeply, rubbing my eyes and unfolding my aching body. I followed the officer into a room where she lectured me about laws and fines. After what seemed like forever, she finally pointed to the station phone. At last. I was free! I could go home! I dialed Tung at our house.

"I'm out of jail!" I said. "Can you pick me up?"

"No!" she said. "Why you no sit inside more?"

I froze, shocked. Was she serious?

"You have to learn. Walk home," Tung told me, then the line went dead.

Bà ác lắm! I thought in Vietnamese. I had learned the phrase from Tung herself: "That lady is cruel!" The station was a good 10 miles [16 km] from our house, clear on the other side of Miami. I had no cash with me, so a taxi was out of the question. So was a bus.

I better start walking, I thought.

Miami was always hot and humid, and I sweated through the long-sleeved shirt and pants I had on from the night before as I made my way home. The knee that had bothered me since I was a teenager grew more painful with each step. As I walked down one block, then the next, I tried to make sense of my anger toward Tung. I thought to myself, *I am the sponsor. She is the refugee. I am supposed to be teaching Tung. Not the other way around.*

I remembered Tung once told me that when she was a child, her grandmother instructed her father, "Don't be hard on Tung." Were those words a reminder for me to be patient with Tung, as well? Objectively, I understood that she had grown up in a very different culture—one that allowed parents to be hard on their children for their mistakes.

I walked south through the city's Cuban neighborhood, hearing the lively jangle of music, the bustle of shopkeepers sweeping the sidewalks and opening their doors for the day. As 3 miles [5 km] became 5 miles [8 km], I thought more about Tung. I was so proud of how far she had come from the traumatized, malnourished, and pregnant woman I had picked up at the Miami airport six years earlier. Now she was driving, cooking in our own restaurant, and raising her beautiful daughter. She no longer shook in terror each time I lit the gas stove. She no longer spent hours crying on my balcony, overwhelmed by the strangeness of my house and this country. Along the way, we had become a family—something I never thought I wanted.

Then my anger returned. I shook my head, thinking, *Don't be hard on Tung? The person who just made me walk home after I spent all night in jail? The person who should have helped me?*

19

"Bả ác lắm!" I said to myself. Vietnamese was the perfect language—so staccato, so abrupt, so to the point. I picked up the pace as I walked past Coral Gables High School, one of the best in the city, and the one I was already dreaming that Phuong Lien would attend. I sweated even more under the midday sun. Finally I arrived at our small home. I walked up to Tung and she looked at me, eyes flashing.

"I hurt," I told her.

"Why don't you walk some more?" she retorted.

I turned away and fell into bed, aching all over. I knew that once I rested, things would be better; I would play with Phuong Lien, eat Tung's delicious phở, and talk with my customers. And Tung and I would go back to trying to understand each other.

CHAPTER 1

My Grandmother's Soup, Part 1

Fort Indiantown Gap Refugee Camp, Lebanon County, PA,
May to August 1975

TUNG:

I followed an American officer into a big, white tent. He pointed me to the cot, then brought his hands together and put them under his head. This is where I would sleep. I then followed him to a large building with lots of tables and one longer table that had food on it. This is where I would eat. He kept saying the word *sponsor,* which was what we refugees needed to leave the camp and settle in America.

I was farther from my tiny village of Điện Bàn in the countryside of central Vietnam, than I had ever imagined. After my father's unexpected death a few years prior, I left home for the first time and took a bus to the big city, Saigon, about 500 miles [800 km] away. There, I sold soup from a market stall and sent money home to help my mother support my six younger siblings. Then, one day in late April 1975, chaos erupted. The Communists were taking over Saigon. I fled from my stall in the market and blindly followed the crowds.

My journey to the United States was a blur. I remember a wooden boat, rocking on the open ocean for what seemed like forever. Vomiting, thirst, rainwater, crying children, dying people. A brief stay in Guam, where we initially landed after being saved by a rescue ship. Helicopters and airplanes. Tents and cots and endless lines of silent Vietnamese people, all of our eyes filled with the same sense of loss.

I only wished I could tell my mother what had happened to me. When she didn't receive money from me, she might think I had died. She might also become so desperate that she would have to sell one of my siblings so that the rest of the family could survive. The very thought filled me with guilt and despair. I was alive, but what did that matter if my family would be torn apart?

I drew my strength from the memory and spirit of my late grandmother Bà Nội. In my mind, I saw Bà Nội's toothless grin, black from chewing betel nut. I pictured her long salt-and-pepper hair wrapped around her head in braids. I thanked her for delivering me here alive, even if everything I knew was gone.

+ + +

Remembering Bà Nội's voice kept me going. It always had. When I was three and stricken with smallpox, my parents were unable to afford medicine. It was Bà Nội who laid me on the dirt floor of her hut and nursed me back to health. As I grew up, always following her around like a baby duck, she looked at my face full of smallpox scars not in horror, as so many others did, but like I was the most beautiful person she had ever seen. When we had only a few grains of rice to eat, Bà Nội taught me to thank God for salt. Rice was just rice, she told me. But if you have rice and salt, you have a meal.

On the days when Bà Nội could spare ginger and pumpkins growing on our farm, we could have a pot of soup, which was practically a feast. I was barely tall enough to reach the pot over the fire when I first watched Bà Nội's wrinkled hands grabbing the ginger and showing me how to cut it into thin slices. I watched as she dropped the thin, fibrous root and chunks of orange pumpkin into the pot of stock that had taken her all day to make by simmering chicken bones in water. I watched because, even though I was just eight years old, I knew I could learn to make the soup myself.

A few months later, when Bà Nội said she trusted me enough to make dinner for the family, I did it myself, my way. I put her knife aside and instead pounded the ginger with a mortar and pestle. I added a tiny bit of rock sugar. I simmered the orange liquid until the fragrance filled the air. Then I invited my grandmother to taste my soup.

Her face lit up. "Oh, my goodness! I can't believe you're my granddaughter," she exclaimed.

+ + +

I didn't understand most of what the Americans in charge of the camp were saying. They were all kind and gentle, though, and that made me feel safe. The thousands of Vietnamese who surrounded me were not nearly as nice to me. As soon as I started speaking, they frowned at the low, heavy tones of my country accent and turned away. They could tell that I was a poor peasant and they didn't want anything to do with me, even though we had all just lost our homes and our country.

It also seemed like everyone at the camp had family with them, or at least one friend. I knew no one. I was completely alone. I felt very, very sad—so much so that I thought about killing myself. Then, a few days after I arrived at the camp, a woman behind me in the lunch line said in Vietnamese, "Where are you from?"

Surprised, I tilted my head and looked at her for a moment. "I'm from Đà Nẵng," I replied. It was the closest city to my village that she might know.

"I'm Bà Hoang," she said. "I am from Hanoi. Would you like to sit with my family?"

Hanoi. Just the word filled me with dread. My family always told me to never trust people from Northern Vietnam, saying they would never respect those of us who lived in the south. But when I looked at Bà Hoang's salt-and-pepper hair, I couldn't help but think of my grandmother. And for now, she was the only Vietnamese person talking to me, so I carried my thin paper plate over to her table. As hungry as I was, I mostly just pushed around the food—a yellow mush they called scrambled eggs, grits or "American chow," and soggy carrots. To me it had no taste, and I missed the familiarity of my beef noodle soup. The Hoangs coaxed me to eat: "You must," they said. "It will keep you strong." I tried a few bites of a crispy meat called bacon and happily found it to be delicious.

The Hoangs and I started to spend a lot of time together, and I started to feel less lonely. Not long after we met, Ông Hoang told me he had invited a friend of his named Minh to eat with us. "He's a good person," he promised.

Minh, a soldier, was from South Vietnam, the region I knew and trusted. I quickly learned that we had something else in common. "I don't have a family," he told me. "Just like you." As soon as he said that, I understood why the Hoangs had introduced us: such typical Vietnamese, trying to match up two lonely people, and without wasting any time.

Cautious, I told both the Hoangs and Minh that we should start out as friends. But, as expected, the Hoangs pushed back. "You need a family," Bà Hoang said. "You can't survive in this country without a family."

"We can all travel together when we leave the camp," added her husband.

I had always been skeptical of marriage. Growing up, I mostly knew it as a business transaction, generally handled by parents and grandparents. And I had seen how women in Vietnam tended to behave after they got married. It was like they became their husband's property. They always walked behind them. They put their husband's needs first. They lived with their in-laws, who set all the house rules. Becoming a wife seemed no different than becoming a servant.

My parents' relationship was not like that, but I knew it was rare. My mother and father always walked side by side. They were equals. My father treated my mother with tenderness, and he never hit her like I'd seen so many of my uncles do to their wives. If I was going to get married, I wanted a marriage like the one my parents had.

After dinner, Minh and I went for a walk alone around the camp. I tried not to look at his smashed nose and his overbite. As we strolled past the rows of neat white buildings and laundry hanging from clotheslines, he said all of the right things. He talked of building a family together, of having each other for support, of making this foreign country less scary if we had each other.

He was very convincing, and I started to put my worries aside. "I don't have anyone," I found myself telling him. "Maybe God sent you so that we could be a family."

After a few of these walks over the next two months, I knew an engagement was expected—by both of us and anyone aware of our relationship. That was always how it worked in Vietnam. By now, I had settled into the idea of marrying Minh. It all made sense. It meant that I would not be alone in this new country, and before long, I would have children. We learned that we could go to an American sponsor's house together, possibly with the Hoangs. I would belong—to someone and to some place.

Minh had brought some gold leaf with him from Vietnam, so we went to the commissary, where he traded it for two gold bands. He handed me one. I held it and watched it sparkle in the sunlight, but for some reason, I didn't put it on my finger.

We went to his tent and made love. It was my first time. Bà Nội had always told me never to sleep with a man before we got married. I had never heard of anyone in my village sleeping with someone before they were married. But I was just so lonely.

I knew I should have felt happy and settled. Instead, I began to have doubts. Was marrying Minh really in my best interest? Maybe Bà Hoang was arranging the relationship just so she could have control over me. Would I have to act like her traditional daughter-in-law? Worse, Minh started to remind me of husbands I had seen in Vietnam: forceful, nothing like my sweet father. The harshness I saw made me regret sleeping with him.

After sundown each evening, it got quite cold at the camp, at least for us Vietnamese, who were used to much warmer temperatures. The traditional tunic-like, thin áo bà ba shirt I had on when I fled Saigon was no match for this weather. The people running the camp started giving out heavy shirts with buttons down the front to help keep us warm. They called them coats. Minh took an armful. One must be for me, I thought.

"Can I have one?" I asked.

He shook his head. "No."

That night, as I sat shivering, I happened to see one of the coats Minh had taken. It was on another woman.

I made up my mind right then and there. The doubts I felt were real. If I went with Minh, he would always treat me as less than him. I was better off asking the Americans to send me somewhere by myself. I would face this country my way.

The next day, I snatched a napkin from the commissary, wrapped it around the ring, and headed across the camp to confront Ông and Bà Hoang.

"You pushed me to go with this guy so that you could have a servant," I yelled as I flung the ring at them, hitting Ông Hoang in the nose. Then I fled. I huddled on my cot and cried for days. At night, I wrapped myself in my blanket, asking Bà Nội to give me strength and help me survive. I avoided Minh and the Hoangs for the rest of my time at the camp.

A few weeks later, a processing agent asked me through a translator where I wanted to resettle. I did not think twice before replying: "Somewhere warm."

Pumpkin Soup (Bí Đỏ) with Fried Shallots

Tung served Hy Vong customers this version of the soup her Bà Nội taught her to make when she was a child. Calabaza squash is also known as West Indian pumpkin. Kabocha or butternut squash are fine substitutes.

SERVES 6 TO 8

9 cups [2.1 L] Hy Vong Stock (page 66), hot or warm

2½ lb [1.2 kg] calabaza squash, seeded, peeled, and cut into 1 in [2.5 mm] cubes (about 8 cups [2 L])

½ small sweet onion, chopped

¼ cup [55 g] crystallized (also known as candied) ginger, minced

¼ cup [60 ml] fish sauce

1 tsp kosher salt

½ tsp Accent Flavor Enhancer (optional)

1½ tsp curry powder

¾ cup [180 ml] heavy cream or coconut milk

4 green onions, thinly sliced, for garnish

½ cup [22 g] Fried Shallots (page 28), for garnish

In a large pot, combine the stock, squash, onion, ginger, fish sauce, salt, and Accent (if using). Bring to a boil over high heat. Lower the heat and simmer, without stirring, until the squash is tender, 5 to 10 minutes. Remove from the heat and stir in the curry powder. Let cool for at least 5 minutes, then stir in the cream. Ladle into bowls and garnish with the green onions and shallots.

Fried Shallots

Crispy fried shallots are a traditional garnish in Vietnam for Pumpkin Soup (Bí Đỏ, page 27), Bánh Cuốn (page 199), and many other dishes. They are best eaten the same day they are fried but will keep, in an airtight container, in the refrigerator for about 1 week.

MAKES ABOUT 1¼ CUPS [55 G]

Vegetable oil, for frying

8 oz [230 g] shallots, cut into ⅛ in [4 mm] rings

Line a plate with paper towels. In a wok or small saucepan, add about 2 in [5 cm] of oil and heat over high heat. When the oil begins to smoke, at about 400°F [200°C], add the shallots, stir a few times with chopsticks or a slotted spoon, then lower the heat to medium. Continue to fry, stirring occasionally, until the shallots are golden brown and crisp, 7 to 10 minutes.

Remove the shallots with a skimmer, letting any excess oil drip back into the wok, and transfer to the paper towel–lined plate to drain. Cool before using.

CHAPTER 2

My Grandmother's Soup, Part 2

Miami, Spring 1975

KATHY:

I watched the television in horror. The end of the Vietnam War had dominated the nightly news for months, looking worse every night. I saw people clawing and kicking and climbing over the fence of the American embassy in Saigon. I heard about the crash of a rescue plane heading out of Vietnam, filled with orphans. I saw families cling together on boats on the rocky ocean after fleeing their country. As a University of Miami graduate student who worked at the school bookstore, I didn't have much extra time or money. But when I saw the terrified faces of those refugees, I wanted to help.

How could I do so? I immediately thought back to my maternal grandmother, Anna Katherine Peterson. I spent long afternoons with her while growing up in small-town Ames, Iowa. A statuesque woman who wore her dark hair in braids wrapped around her head, she filled her days cooking, fixing up homes, and playing with her many foster children. Grandma Peterson taught me to always help others—even if they were different from us. She knew what it was like to need help. As a teenager, she and her family moved to the United States from Sweden. She married and had two daughters, but lost the oldest, Margarita, to polio and pneumonia. Grandma's marriage wasn't happy, either: She endured years of physical and verbal abuse from her husband, who finally abandoned the family when my mother, Gwendolyn, was thirteen.

In a way, that's where Grandma's story really began. She found a job cleaning at Iowa State University and raised my mother on her own. Even with this hardship, she also became a successful entrepreneur who saved enough money to purchase three houses and turn them into rental properties. She always looked for ways to help others with her money rather than spend it on herself. She never worried about her own financial situation: She always believed that God would take care of her.

Grandma took in boys and girls who had lived in dangerous or abusive situations and had nowhere else to stay. She eventually fostered a total of 125 children over her lifetime, including one boy named Charles, who came for a few weeks and ended up staying for thirteen years. He became one of my closest friends. And she was always feeding strangers who knocked on her back door. At one point, she was sending food, clothes, and money to a struggling Norwegian family with six children, even though Grandma Peterson was Swedish and the two groups of immigrants did not always get along.

The home she created—full of children and good food— became a haven for me when I was growing up. I was a chubby child who refused to wear dresses and would rather clean horse stalls than chase boys. I felt so out of place when my sisters discussed makeup and high heels and their future husbands. I knew I was expected to get married and have children, but to me this seemed so unappealing—I regarded it as an endless series of chores. As such, many people in Ames looked at me as if something were wrong with me, and my mother worried constantly about my fate.

Not Grandma. She showed me only love and acceptance. She taught me that my differences made me special. She showed me how our deep faith meant that we should help everyone in need.

I loved crowding around the table in Grandma's kitchen with my siblings and Grandma's foster children, watching her open packages of dried prunes and apricots and raisins, knowing that her Swedish fruit soup was in the making. As the prunes slowly softened in a bubbling pot, Grandma filled her pink flowered pitcher with heavy cream. After the fruit soup cooled, we took turns pouring cream into our bowls and watching it swirl around the darkened fruit.

+ + +

My family moved to Miami in 1960, at the start of my sophomore year of high school. Though its Latin culture and swaying palm trees had come as a shock to someone who had grown up in a mostly Caucasian town in the Midwest, I eventually came to love its ethnic diversity and exuberance. After graduating, I completed two years at a local community college, then worked and traveled and worked some more before eventually finishing my bachelor's degree in sociology at Miami's Barry University in 1973. I was twenty-eight years old and again found myself at a crossroads, trying to figure out what to do with my life.

Two years later, I began studying for my teaching degree at the University of Miami, where I also worked in the bookstore. I lived in my parents' empty house in the Coconut Grove section of Miami; they had just moved to my older sister's farm in Virginia. I was lonely in the two-story, three-bedroom house, so I was delighted when my longtime friend Thao came to live with me in February 1975. She had grown up in Đà Nẵng, in central Vietnam, and her wealthy family had sent her to the United States to attend college at Barry, which is where we met.

Thao usually bounced around with infectious energy and swinging shoulder-length black hair, cooking sticky rice and

Chinese sausage and chattering away. But that changed as the situation in her home country became increasingly grim. Thao grew quiet and ate less and less. She began dialing her parents and siblings several times a day. At first the phone would ring and ring, but no one would answer. Then her calls wouldn't even go through.

The night we heard David Brinkley report on NBC that Đà Nẵng had fallen to the North Vietnamese Army, we watched coverage of the bedlam at the Đà Nẵng airport, crowds of people pushing and struggling to climb onto the last flights out. We assumed—well, we hoped—that Thao's family was somewhere in that sea of fleeing people. They had the money and the connections to leave Vietnam.

A few days later, Thao's twenty-eight-year-old brother, Huong, called with an update: The family had all run to the airport together, but he was the only one who managed to get on a flight. It landed in Saigon, and now he needed an American sponsor in order to go to the States.

I didn't even think twice. "Of course I'll sponsor him," I said. I wanted to do whatever I could to help.

Two months later, we were at the Miami airport waiting for Huong to arrive. I thought about how he and all the other refugees may have been luckier than those left behind, but their reward was bittersweet and involved a new, unknown life. I had never been in a situation like theirs, but I knew what it was like to feel different, disoriented. I knew how it felt not to belong.

I didn't have much money or time, but I did have a big, empty house. Maybe there was a way I could help even more.

Swedish Fruit Soup

Grandma Peterson served this soup all year long, and at all times of day. She usually started it the night before, but as long as the fruit can soak for about 8 hours before cooking, you can make the entire recipe in a day. For the best results, follow Grandma Peterson's method and avoid stirring the soup so the fruits stay whole. The flavors will blend together as the mixture simmers.

SERVES 4 TO 6

1 lb [455 g] dried prunes, dried apricots, and dried apples
(in whatever proportions you like)

½ cup [100 g] sugar

½ cup [70 g] golden raisins

2 thin slices of lemon

2 cinnamon sticks

6 whole cloves

¼ tsp kosher salt

¼ cup [30 g] minute tapioca

About 2 cups [480 ml] heavy cream, for drizzling

In a medium pot, combine the dried fruit with 5 cups [1.2 L] of water. Cover and let sit, at room temperature, until the fruit is very plump, 8 to 12 hours.

Add the sugar, raisins, lemon, cinnamon sticks, cloves, salt, and 1 cup [240 ml] of water. Do not stir the mixture. Cover the pot and bring the liquid to a boil over high heat. Lower the heat and simmer, without stirring, for about 15 minutes. Sprinkle the tapioca on top of the fruit, then use a wooden spoon to lightly push down on the fruit to submerge the tapioca. Again,

continued

do not stir the soup. Cover the pot and simmer for 5 minutes more. Remove the lid and let the soup cool for at least 15 minutes. Refrigerate, if you want to serve the soup cold.

Before serving, remove and discard the cinnamon sticks and cloves. Serve warm or cold, drizzled with as much heavy cream as you like. The soup will keep, tightly covered, in the refrigerator for up to 3 days.

CHAPTER 3
Brand New

Miami, Summer and Fall 1975

TUNG:

So fast!

We sped through Miami. I thought we might crash. I tried to hold on to the edge of my seat. Sights flew by: huge buildings, shiny cars, enormous trucks. Where were the bicycles and the three-wheeled rickshaws that I knew from Vietnam?

So much noise!

Americans talked so loud! During the drive to her house, Kathy smiled a lot, but it sounded like she was yelling at me every time she spoke.

So bright!

Why were there lights everywhere? It was night, but it looked just like daytime.

So alone.

+ + +

My trip had begun at an airport near the camp in Pennsylvania.

"Where am I going?" I asked the driver.

"A place called Florida," he said. "It is warm, like Vietnam. You're going to live with an American with two dogs."

My eyes widened. The dogs lived with the American? Inside the house? Why?

I shook in terror as I walked off the plane in Miami, following the crowds of people, not sure where I was going. I was relieved to see a Vietnamese man waiting for me at the gate.

"Hello," he said in Vietnamese, with a polished, educated accent. "I am Huong. Say hi to Kathy," he said, pointing to a fat American woman with yellow hair. "We are all going to live in Kathy's house. My sister Thao also lives there."

Right away, Kathy started her yelling and smiling. As we walked to her car, I noticed how her hair frizzled around her head. So different than my own straight black hair. After our scary twenty-minute car ride, we pulled into a driveway and my heart started to pound.

This could not be a house! It was larger than any house I had ever seen. And with its bright white stucco, big wooden front door, and big round window, it looked just like the Christian churches in Saigon. Vietnamese believe that the spirits of dead people stay on earth inside churches. Was I going to be living in a place filled with ghosts?

I slowly followed Kathy and Huong into the house. Kathy pressed something and I squinted as the room filled with light. Too much light. She showed me around. In a bathroom, she turned a handle and said a word in English: "faucet." Water came right out! In another room, I saw what looked to be a very soft bed. This was where I would be sleeping. It was so different from the bamboo mats I was used to.

When I woke up the next morning, I wondered what I would do with myself now. I needed to keep moving. I needed to forget. I noticed a lot of leaves outside the house, so I asked Huong for a broom. Next, I washed my clothes, as I always had, outside in a pan of water. I wrung them out and hung them on the clothesline to dry.

What I really wanted to do was cook. I didn't understand America, but I understood how to make food. Maybe I could gather some sticks and build a fire outdoors. That was the only way I had ever cooked. Instead, Kathy guided me into a room in the house that she called a kitchen. She turned a knob, and I heard a BOOM! I jumped as a circle of flames erupted. Were we in danger?! Then I realized that Kathy was smiling. "Stove," she said. A fire inside the house—this was how Americans cooked. Amazing! Kathy walked me over to a tall box and opened a door. Cold air filled the room. I had no idea air could be so cold. "Refrigerator," she said.

I was so confused by this kitchen, and I didn't really like the food. Kathy cooked something she called "hamburgers." It was meat inside bread—too much bread. I took off the top part and ate the meat with the lettuce, tomato, and onion.

A few days later, I thought I would cook something for Kathy, Huong, and Thao. I looked in the refrigerator but did not see vegetables. "Go to the store," Huong said. He took out some American money and gave me what he said was $15. He pointed me down the street to a small grocery store.

When I went inside, I couldn't believe how clean it was. I sniffed and sniffed, but could not smell any of the fish or meat like at the markets in Vietnam. And here you could get everything you needed, indoors at one place. I gazed at all the fruits, vegetables, metal cans, and brightly colored boxes. I saw all the customers pushing around big, shiny metal carts with wheels. I grabbed one and did the same. I picked out meat, watercress, green onions, onions, lettuce, and tomatoes—what I needed to make bò lúc lắc, sautéed beef and salad. Paying for the groceries was easy, and soon I was back home in the kitchen.

And then my hands took over. They seemed to move by themselves, as they always did when food was involved. I sliced the green onions, chopped the onions, washed the lettuce and tomatoes. Tossing them together, sautéing the steak, moving, moving, made me feel like the world made sense again. All the terrible images from my journey to America flew out of my head for a few quiet minutes.

I put the food on the dining room table for Kathy, Thao, and Huong, then snuck upstairs and onto a balcony that looked out on the front yard. I knew I could not eat with them. They were wealthier, more important people. I was not one of them. I knew I should disappear.

Now that my hands were still, I began to cry again. I saw Minh's smashed nose, Mrs. Hoang's salt-and-pepper hair. I heard the screams in Saigon and felt the sting of the ocean water in the boat. I wondered whether my mother had already tried to sell my youngest brothers.

I looked around at the yard, full of trees and flowers I did not recognize. My shoulders hunched as I heard Kathy yelling my name from somewhere in the house. I spoke again to Bà Nội. "Maybe you sent me to the wrong place," I said. "I don't know what to do."

KATHY:

I had rarely tasted anything so delicious. Tender meat, fresh green onions, salad with a light and tangy dressing. I couldn't stop eating. But where was the person who had cooked this food? I called for her.

"Where's Tung? Tung? *Tung!*"

Day after day, that scene kept repeating itself. This tiny woman, her terrified face marred by pockmarks and streaked by tears, would stop shaking long enough to cook something delicious. Then she'd put the meal on the table and vanish. I called her name over and over, hoping that she would come eat dinner with the rest of us.

I gave up because I wanted to eat! My house had turned into the best restaurant I had ever experienced. I slurped steaming bitter melon soup and wolfed down chicken and ginger, pork belly with green tomatoes, and spicy ribs. I wondered what kind of life this woman had lived before she landed in America, and where she learned how to cook like this. If only she spoke English.

Tung looked at everything with such wide, scared eyes; everything was new to her. The flowers outside my window! The park! The windows and mirrors of my car! I took her to Sears to buy clothes, and she shrank back from the bright store lights and her mouth fell open as she gazed at all the racks of pants and shirts and dresses. Then we got to the escalator.

Tung looked at the moving metal stairs. Then she looked at her feet. She picked up one foot, put it down, then picked up the other. She didn't know where to place them. It was as if she was marching in place. I grabbed ahold of her thin arm and pulled her onto the bottom stair. Tung clung tightly to me. Her legs quaked so much I feared they might buckle any minute and send her toppling down the escalator. She surprised me by standing steady as we rose to the second floor.

+ + +

I felt terrible that Tung looked so scared. But I was having so much fun with her, watching her experience everything for the first time with such gentle, childlike wonderment. In fact, I was having so much fun that it took me a while to realize that Thao, my longtime friend and confidante, who spoke fluent Vietnamese, was ignoring Tung. For that matter, Thao didn't understand why I would want to get to know Tung, either. "She will never understand what you are telling her," Thao said.

As I tried to process this, I got a call from my pastor at St. James Lutheran Church. I had volunteered to host Tung through the church, which worked with Lutheran World Relief—Tung's official sponsor to come to the United States. Now, my pastor asked if I had room for more refugees that the international nonprofit organization was sponsoring. I was not receiving money to host any of these refugees, but I didn't think twice about that when I told my pastor, "Of course."

The next thing I knew, I was driving to the airport again to pick up a big family: two parents, a grandmother, five children, and two cousins. Now Thao and I were living with a total of twelve Vietnamese refugees. I let the family take over the upstairs of my house. Tung, Thao, Huong, and I could sleep on blankets on the living room floor. I was just so happy to have a house full of people. I loved the noise and the activity and the big meals in the dining room. I assumed all of the Vietnamese would talk to each other—after all, they were from the same country and spoke the same language.

I had so much to learn.

Over the next two weeks, I discovered that the group of refugees in my house was an unlikely bunch. They represented completely different Vietnamese classes and cultures, and probably never would have encountered each other if they were in Vietnam. Now that they were in America, they still had no intention of mixing with each other.

The differences were stark from the beginning. While Tung entered my house with a single tattered bag that contained a few clothes, the family made a grand entrance with a load of expensive-looking suitcases. We had to make five trips to the airport to pick up all of their luggage, and one suitcase even contained a television set! Hours after they arrived, I found the two cousins, Luc and Tay, busy ironing the family's long silk dresses.

"Wow, the cousins work so hard!" I said to Thao.

It would take a few more weeks before I realized that Luc and Tay were actually servants, poor people who had been sold to the wealthy family. They posed as cousins in hopes of coming to America with their employers.

One day after work, I walked into the garage and found Tung sitting on the ground, shoulders hunched, crying. "What's wrong?" I asked. She pointed to the marks on her face. After a lot of frantic hand motions, I figured out that the family had blamed her for giving one of their sons chicken pox from her pockmarks, and she believed them. She didn't realize that wasn't possible.

They were bullying Tung because she was poor and from the countryside. When I talked about their behavior with Thao, who also came from an upper-class family, she saw nothing wrong with their behavior. She also said she thought Tung was stupid because she was a poor peasant.

That was when I became angry. Tung was definitely not stupid. I saw the way she watched and listened to me, trying to understand everything I did and said. She had begun to learn many English words; not surprisingly, *fork*, *spoon*, and *knife* were among the first. Tung also never stopped working. The house and yard had never been more spotless. By contrast, no one from the family ever tried to learn or do anything. They just sat around all day.

And when it came to cooking, Tung was brilliant. It was also the only thing that made her smile. Her cooking made me happy, too. I liked peeking into the kitchen and seeing her there, wrapping up spring rolls or stirring a pot of simmering soup. I had learned to intercept her before she snuck upstairs and insisted that she sit down and eat with us.

When Tung started saying "phở" a few weeks into her stay with me, I realized she wanted to make the traditional Vietnamese soup I once had during a trip to Washington D.C. Excited to eat phở in my own home, I took Tung to a nearby Asian grocery store. Fortunately she found the necessary rice noodles and fish sauce, and some beef and pork bones for the stock. She had already rummaged through the pantry and found a packet of star anise, which my mother used to flavor iced tea.

After a few hours at the stove, she summoned all of us for dinner. I sat down to a magical soup: rich, anise-flavored broth filled

41

with silky noodles, thin slices of sweet onion and beef tenderloin, lots of herbs, and a wedge of lime. I looked up from my soup reverie. The big family said nothing, though they were slurping away every last drop. I expected to see Tung smiling back at me. Instead, she was peering into her bowl, shaking her head in disgust.

"No good," she said.

I shook my head back in confusion. How could she not love this soup? What could possibly be wrong?

Unable to argue with her, I ended up taking her back to the store a few days later. I watched her prowl around the aisles more carefully this time and suddenly saw her light up. In front of her was a refrigerated case full of other types of bones: marrowbones cut into cylinders, beef knuckles, turkey wings, pig's feet, beef feet. She bought more bones than I thought could possibly fit into the pot.

Her second broth was thicker, stronger, richer. "This is even more delicious!" I told her. This time, Tung didn't glare at me. Her small face broke into a wide smile.

A few mornings later, I was surprised when I woke up and didn't find her in the kitchen. I heard the sound of retching coming from the bathroom. I walked over and found Tung kneeling over the toilet. She gestured to her stomach with a dismayed look. I had picked up some Vietnamese by then and recognized the words for "once a month." I realized she was telling me she had missed her period.

"Oh, boy," I said.

Phở

Over the years, Tung tweaked her phở until she was satisfied with this version, which the *Miami New Times* named the city's best phở in 2013. It is easier to cut the beef knuckle meat if it's cold, so if you have time, chill it after the initial cooking. Tung likes to cut the onion as described below because it results in more pungent slices—a plus for this soup. Phở noodles come in three different sizes; Tung prefers the medium-width. Don't worry about putting the raw tenderloin on top of the noodles, as the slices will cook when you pour the hot stock over them.

This recipe makes a big batch; you can freeze leftover stock for up to 3 months.

SERVES 8 TO 10

STOCK

3 lb [1.4 kg] boneless beef knuckle, top or bottom round, or sirloin, fat trimmed

2 lb [910 g] beef short ribs or beef neck or soup bones

1½ lb [680 g] chicken backs or necks

1½ lb [680 g] beef marrowbones or oxtail

1½ lb [680 g] pork neck bones

1 turkey leg (about 1½ lb [680 g])

1 medium sweet onion, chopped

¼ cup [60 ml] fish sauce, plus more as needed

3 large whole star anise

1 Tbsp sugar

1 Tbsp kosher salt

1 tsp Accent Flavor Enhancer (optional)

continued

43

SOUP

½ large sweet onion, halved lengthwise
and thinly sliced crosswise

1 bunch basil, leaves chopped

1 bunch cilantro, leaves chopped

1 bunch green onions, thinly sliced

2 lb [910 g] bean sprouts

2 lb [910 g] flat dried rice noodles, labeled "Bánh Phở,"
cooked according to package directions

8 oz [230 g] beef tenderloin, sliced against the
grain as thinly as possible (optional)

2 limes, cut into wedges, for garnish

TO MAKE THE STOCK:

Rinse the beef knuckle, beef short ribs, chicken backs, marrowbones, pork neck bones, and turkey leg under cold running water, removing any bone fragments. In a large pot, combine the bones, meat, and 7 qt [6.6 L] of cold water and bring to a boil over high heat. Skim any scum off the surface, stir, then lower the heat and gently simmer, without mixing or skimming, for 3½ hours. You should have between 5 and 6 qt [4.7 and 5.7 L] of stock. If necessary, add water to reach 5 qt [4.7 L]; continue to simmer if you have more than 6 qt [5.7 L].

Off the heat, skim any scum, then remove all the bones and meat. Set aside the beef knuckle and short ribs; discard the chicken and pork bones, marrowbones or oxtail, and the turkey leg. Return the stock to high heat and add the sweet onion, fish sauce, star anise, sugar, salt, and Accent (if using). Cut any visible fat off the beef knuckle, then cut the meat with the grain into rectangular pieces about 3 in [7.5 cm] wide. Cut each of these into ¼ in [6 mm] thick slices against the grain. Add the meat to the pot. Cut some of the meat off the short ribs, thinly slice, and add to the pot.

Bring the stock to a boil, without stirring, then turn off the heat. Let sit for 10 to 15 minutes so the fat can rise to the top. Skim any fat and scum off the surface. Taste the stock; if you'd like a more savory or saltier flavor, and add more fish sauce or salt.

TO MAKE THE SOUP:

In a large bowl, toss together the sweet onion, basil, cilantro, and green onions, and set aside. To serve, set out ten deep soup bowls and put about 1 cup [100 g] of bean sprouts in each, crushing them lightly with your fingers. Top each with about 1½ cups [100 g] of the noodles, a few slices of the tenderloin (if using), some knuckle meat and short rib meat, and 2 to 3 cups [480 to 720 ml] of the stock. Divide the onion-herb mixture among the bowls and garnish with the lime wedges.

CHAPTER 4
Rice and Salt

Miami, Fall 1975 to March 1976

TUNG:

I had never done anything that my grandmother would not have been happy about, either during her life or after she died. I always caught the most fish, grew the best rice, cooked the most delicious meals. When others made Bà Nội sad or angry, her eyes would widen, her cheeks would puff out, and she'd need to go for a walk by herself. But that anger was never about me.

Now I had slept with a man without us being married, and I was having his baby. Alone.

I'm sorry, Bà Nội.

Kathy took me to what she called a "charity hospital" to see a doctor. After we waited for hours in crowded rooms, the doctor examined me, told me that I was having a baby, and asked Kathy some questions. Kathy shook her head at one question, but the doctor kept talking. Finally, Kathy put her hand on mine and told

46

me that the doctor was asking if I wanted to take my baby out. I shook my head. She smiled at me and told the doctor "no."

Later, Kathy told me that that hospital was no place to have a baby, so she had found "the best doctor in town" for me. On the day of my appointment, Kathy had to work, so Thao took me. Since Thao spoke English, the doctor spoke only to her as they both looked at me. I didn't understand more than a few words, and Thao wasn't translating for me, so I kept quiet, even though I had questions of my own.

In the car, Thao began speaking to me in Vietnamese, telling me what she and the doctor had discussed. The word *abortion* was new to me, but I now understood why she and the doctor kept looking at me. They did not feel I should have a child because I was poor and alone. "Now, you have to think about this," Thao said. "You have to take out your baby."

My anger grew as we drove home. Why should anyone tell me what to do with my baby? I knew I was a peasant and it was not my place to fight more educated people, but this time I had to talk back. As hard as it was, I had to stand up to someone with more status.

We pulled into Kathy's driveway. At last, I opened my mouth. "Why did you tell me that? Why did you tell me to take my baby out?" I could see Thao's eyes growing wide. She was shocked that I would argue with her. She looked so mad that I wondered whether she might even hurt me.

I jumped out of the car and slammed the door as hard as I could. Thao also stepped out of the car. "I don't care if you're mad," I told her. "Don't ask me that again." What had been done was done. I had to keep going. I had to take care of my child.

"As long I have rice and salt," I declared, "I will keep my baby."

+++

I climbed the steps to Kathy's balcony and spoke to the spirit of Bà Nội. "I did not mean to bring shame to the family," I said

47

out loud as the tears began to flow. "I did not mean to have sex before being married. I did not mean to get pregnant. I was just so lonely and scared."

Now I had another thing to fear: that my baby would look like Minh. I thought that God might punish me by giving me a baby with his nose and overbite who would always remind me of that man. Every day I pleaded with Trời (God): "Please forgive me. Please let my baby look like my family."

Each day, as I stood on the balcony, worrying about the future, I looked at a tall tree with fanlike leaves. I watched as its red flowers began to emerge. On the day they began to stretch out their long, delicate petals, I exclaimed, "Americans have phuong, too!" I was so happy to see that it was the same tree I had admired on the streets in Saigon: the phoenix tree, or *phuong*. Kathy later told me that in America they called it the royal poinciana.

In all this strangeness, this tree gave me comfort and familiarity and strength. It was once a young tree, planted in new soil. Now it had grown higher than Kathy's roof, its red flowers providing cover for the yard and the house. I began to think of myself as a tree, too: a young tree, planted in new soil in the land of America. Now that I had water and dirt, I, too, would grow—roots, branches, and soon, the first young leaf.

KATHY:

No one told me what had happened when Thao took Tung to the doctor. I assumed everything was fine. So, because I had to work, I asked Thao to take her to the next appointment, too. This time, Tung saw another doctor and came home weeping. When I took her to her next appointment myself, the nurse told me the doctor had criticized Tung for not speaking English and apologized for him.

Once again, Tung was not getting a square deal, and once again, I got angry about it. American doctors looked down their noses at her because she was a poor, single refugee who didn't speak English. If Tung wanted to keep her baby, I wanted to help her. I just needed to figure out the best way to do that.

I called my sister Anne, who was helping resettle Vietnamese refugees in her home state of Illinois. She told me the first step was to go to the welfare office and fill out the proper forms to get health care coverage for Tung's delivery, the most expensive part of the pregnancy. Fortunately, Tung was able to pay for her prenatal appointments because she now had a job. She was washing dishes in one of the cafeterias at the University of Miami, where I worked and was going to school.

That eventually led to a better-paying job washing dishes eight hours a day at a restaurant near my house called the Rusty Pelican. She was making about $280 a week, which wasn't bad in those days. And when the kitchen was shorthanded, the manager showed her how to clean shrimp, peel onions, and do other prep work. Little did he know that she was probably the most talented cook there.

Despite her pregnancy and forty-hour workweek, Tung still insisted on cleaning my entire house and cooking for all of us. Her first dessert impressed me just as much as her other food: a flan made with sweetened condensed milk. The choice surprised me, as she had so far not seemed interested in dairy products or sweets. As I discovered, though, flan was a common dessert in Vietnam because of its history as a French colony. Tung had learned how to make it when she lived in Saigon. She steamed her flan on the stove top, the same way she had always done it in Saigon. She also added a twist, infusing the caramel sauce with julienned ginger, which complemented the richness of the custard perfectly.

+++

As 1975 turned into 1976, my house began to empty out. Thao moved in with her boyfriend. Huong got a job and left. Luc and Tay broke free of the big family and got their own apartment in another part of Miami. The family spent a ridiculous few weeks

ORY
RICE AND SALT

trying to get me to move out of my parents' house so they could live there alone. When they realized that wouldn't work, they moved to a community of Vietnamese refugees in California. Soon, only Tung and I were left.

Tung had been scheduled to leave for a job that I had gotten for her as a live-in housekeeper for an American family who attended my church in Miami. But they rescinded the offer when they found out she was pregnant. I enjoyed Tung's company and was happy for her to stay with me for as long as she liked.

By March, Tung was nearing her due date. I had learned that she had never been to a hospital or even seen a medical doctor or a dentist until she came to the United States. When I took her to the dentist for the first time, he could not find a single cavity. I had also taken her to every prenatal appointment since that last one with Thao. We spent a lot of time sitting in waiting rooms full of uncomfortable furniture and women with growing bellies, and we talked a lot, too. I always spoke to Tung in proper, not broken, English, and complete sentences, not fragments. She was understanding more and more, and working hard on her pronunciation.

I, too, was learning a new language. I would repeat words or phrases Tung used, and read from my English to Vietnamese dictionary. I didn't really know the difference between all the accents, but I didn't care and neither did she. Tung never laughed at my attempts to say things, even when I confused chúc mừng năm mới ("Happy New Year") with chúc mừng mũi mới ("happy new nose").

Before long, our talks turned to faith. Though our religions were different, it was clear that we both believed in a loving God who saw and knew everything. "Trời có mắt," she would say, pointing to the sky. I'd nod and respond with the English translation, "God has eyes," which reminded me of my Christian upbringing and Grandma Peterson.

Tung told me about her being a Buddhist and the spirits of her dead father and grandmother, and how she wondered whether ghosts lived in my house because it so closely resembled the churches in Saigon. She asked me not to laugh. I promised I would not. Actually, I found it more fascinating than funny. I had never thought of my house in that way before.

+ + +

To our relief, Tung's health benefits were finalized the day before she went into labor, which meant the baby could be delivered at Baptist Hospital—a much better option than the original hospital we had visited. However, after her water broke and she was admitted, we were horrified to see that the obstetrician on call was the doctor who had criticized Tung for not speaking English.

I confronted him. "You are not going to deliver this baby," I told him. "Call her regular doctor."

He left, made some phone calls, and came back to say he had to deliver the baby because Tung's regular doctor was not available. He apologized for his previous behavior. Then, without giving us an explanation, he said he was going to do a cesarean section. Tung was deep into labor by then, and I knew we had no choice but to go along with his decision.

I paced and paced the waiting room, too anxious to sit down. An expectant father was doing the same thing. I laughed to myself, thinking, *I have no idea what I'm doing, either.* After about three hours, a nurse approached me.

"It's a girl," she told me with a smile. She then directed me to the nursery. Among the sea of wrinkled, screaming babies, I spotted Tung's daughter right away through the window. She was perfectly calm. Her eyes were closed, but her hands stretched out in a salute, as if she were announcing, "Here I am!" I had never seen such a beautiful baby.

Another nurse led me to Tung's bed in the recovery area. She woke up when she heard us.

"Baby born rồi?" she asked. I knew this meant, "Has the baby been born already?"

"Yes," I replied. "Tung, it's a girl."

51

She smiled like I had never seen her smile before—a wide, joyful grin. Then she closed her eyes and fell back asleep.

When Tung woke up again, she gave her daughter a first name in honor of her favorite flowering tree, and a middle name that means "lotus," in honor of the water lilies in Vietnam: Phuong Lien.

Flan with Ginger

Tung still makes this flan the same way she learned in Vietnam: on the stove top—not in the oven, which is the more traditional method. For this recipe, you will need a stove-proof 9 in [23 cm] metal baking pan, either a 12 in [30.5 cm] steamer with a metal rack or a lidded wok or deep pot at least 12 in [30.5 cm] wide, and a small heatproof cup or trivet.

SERVES 6 TO 8

¼ cup [50 g] sugar

½ oz [15 g] julienned ginger (from a piece about ¾ in [2 cm] long)

6 large or 5 extra-large eggs

One 14 oz [400 g] can sweetened condensed milk (save the can to measure water)

In the stove-proof baking pan, combine the sugar, ginger, and ⅓ cup [80 ml] of water, and stir until the sugar is dissolved. Bring the mixture to a roiling boil over high heat, then lower the heat and simmer, constantly and very carefully stirring the mixture or swirling the pan. (Use an oven mitt or tongs to hold the side of the pan and swirl slowly.)

After about 5 minutes, the mixture will foam, then turn a mahogany brown and begin to thicken. Keep gently stirring or swirling just until the mixture is deep brown, thick, and gooey, 2 to 3 minutes more, being careful not to burn the caramel. Remove from the heat immediately and let cool slightly, making sure the ginger is evenly scattered across the bottom of the pan.

In a large bowl, whisk the eggs until uniformly yellow, with no whites visible. Continue whisking while slowly adding the condensed milk. When the mixture is thoroughly combined, repeat with 2½ cans of water (measuring the water in the can will help dislodge any milk stuck to the sides), then set the custard aside.

continued

53

If using a steamer, add enough water so that it almost reaches the rack. If using a wok or pot, put the cup or trivet in the bottom and add enough water so it almost reaches the top of the cup or trivet. Carefully put the pan with the caramel on the steamer rack or on top of the cup or trivet. Slowly pour the condensed milk mixture over the caramel, then cover the steamer or wok. Bring the water to a boil over high heat.

When the water comes to a boil (look for steam coming out from under the lid or quickly lift the lid to check), lower the heat so the water simmers. Cook the flan until the edges are set and starting to bubble, and the middle is jiggly, 5 to 6 minutes. You can insert a chopstick or cake tester into the center of the flan to double-check its doneness; it should come out clean.

Carefully remove the pan from the steamer or wok and let it cool. Cover the pan and refrigerate for at least 4 hours, but preferably overnight. To serve, run a knife around the flan; firmly hold a round, rimmed platter or pie dish against the top of the pan; and flip the pan over to invert the flan onto the platter. Slice into wedges and serve with the caramel sauce spooned over the top.

CHAPTER 5

Make More

Miami, March 1976

TUNG:

Kathy and I spent hours looking at my daughter. Phuong Lien was born with a perfectly round head and curious dark eyes. She also had a straight nose and showed no signs of Minh's ugly face. She looked just like my sister, Hiem, who had been born right after my father's death. That meant God had forgiven me. *Thank you, Trời.*

Kathy seemed so happy to have a baby in her house, and that meant a lot to me. She asked many questions about how I had grown up and about my family. She seemed very interested in hearing about Bà Nội, and I was slowly learning enough English to tell her more and more.

A few weeks after I got home from the hospital, I decided it was time to show Kathy the only item I had brought from Vietnam that meant anything to me: my grandmother's ring, a beautiful golden band with a bright-pink ruby stone. I had kept it in a special pocket in my pants during the entire journey from Saigon to the States.

Kathy gasped when I opened my hand. Her eyes looked at me with so many questions. "A lot of love," she finally said. I nodded.

+ + +

Điện Bàn, Central Vietnam: 1948 to 1956

I knelt on the dirt floor in Bà Nội's home, a one-room windowless hut made of mud and stalks from the rice paddies. I squinted in the dark and could just make out two squirming black eels in my grandmother's hands. I knew that Bà Nội might not eat that day because she had used what money she could scrape together to buy the eels and that my only food might be a few grains of rice.

I was three years old. Smallpox had taken over my body, and I could see only bumps where I used to see skin. I itched all the time. I missed my mother and father. They were busy at home, tending to my baby brother Mau, who had also been stricken with the disease. They focused on Mau because as a boy in Vietnamese society, his health was much more important than mine. So I was sent to my grandmother's, a few huts away. Chances were, neither Mau nor I would survive. Smallpox had already killed many people in our village, and it was particularly deadly for families like ours that had no money for medical care and not one, but two desperately sick children.

Bà Nội was helpless to stop the disease that might leave me paralyzed, disfigured, or dead. In the countryside, we could not afford Western medicine. We depended on ancient Chinese medicine and natural herbs. Bà Nội could rely only on rumors handed down by other village women about what might help. First she tried to stop the itch by rubbing my skin with the leaves of rau răm, Vietnamese coriander. Then she went in search of live eel, which apparently could save me from going blind.

She told me to sit still, then slowly rubbed the black eels over my eyes until the creatures went slack and died. Their cool skin sent chills through me. I longed to go out in the sun, but Bà Nội shook her head. She went to bury the eels because she'd been told it was bad luck to eat them. She insisted that I had to sit alone in the dark. No, I didn't! I dug my finger into the wall, jabbing away at the dirt and rice-paddy stalks until I had carved out a tiny hole. It let in a thin stream of sunlight that made me feel less alone.

After a few weeks, my skin felt less like it was on fire. I told this to Bà Nội. She looked deep into my eyes.

"Can you see me?" she asked.

"Yes," I said.

"How many fingers am I holding up?" she asked.

"Five," I answered.

"Now, you're okay!" she exclaimed.

Bà Nội filled a pan with water and told me to look into it. I peered at my reflection in the shimmering water. I could see marks on my face, but she pointed out that the scarring was not deep. I had yet to learn that smallpox had left Mau blind, despite the same treatment. I also had yet to realize the deep concern my grandmother still had for me and my face. She worried that because I was covered in pockmarks, I would always be treated badly by others.

At that moment, I was just happy that I could leave the darkness of Bà Nội's hut. I picked myself up off the floor and padded outside on my bare feet, ready to see the sunshine again.

+++

Our village, Điện Bàn, just outside the city of Đà Nẵng, sat 500 miles [800 km] south of Hanoi and 500 miles north of Saigon. I knew those cities only by name. My family never went anywhere we couldn't reach by walking. We lived on one side of a vast river. On the other side we rented a relatively small piece of land, measuring about 125 by 40 feet [38 by 12 m], where we farmed rice, tobacco, and vegetables. We mainly ate only what we could grow or barter at the market, and many days that was not enough to fill our growling bellies. We slept on bamboo cots. Our only light came from the sun and the moon, not the kerosene lamps that richer people had. Our water came from nearby streams, and we relieved ourselves in a hole dug outside our hut.

Anyone who was unlucky to be different in any way was treated harshly by everyone else. Because Mau went blind at the age of eight months, the village leaders refused to give him a citizenship certificate. Our parents paid for me to go to school the same as other parents paid for their kids, but we were still not treated equally; even our teachers judged students by how they looked.

When I was five, I forgot to add an accent when spelling a word in class. My teacher looked at my pockmarks and responded by reaching for a pile of bricks. He placed several on my shoulders and made me stand in the corner for hours like that. My body ached and tears of shame ran down my face, but I did not get any sorry looks from the other children. After the teacher removed the bricks and sent me home, I told Bà Nội I was not going back to school.

She let me skip two months before sending me back. "Education is precious," she said. "It's an opportunity." On the day I returned, I walked quietly into the one-room hut and sat down to listen to the lesson. I suppose I wasn't sitting still enough because the same teacher approached me with a stick. I heard loud thwacks and at the same time felt a burning pain run through both of my hands.

I stood up, walked out of school, and never returned. From then on I looked to Bà Nội as the teacher of everything I needed to know, particularly when it came to food.

At home, I watched her cut sweet potatoes and yuca into big chunks and cook them over a fire to serve with *mắm tôm*, a fermented shrimp paste. At the market, I listened to her bargain and watched as she looked carefully at each fruit and vegetable she wanted to buy, turning it over in her hand looking for bruises or holes.

When I wasn't with Bà Nội, I spent most of my time tending to our farm. Mostly, women and children did the farming. Men, including my father, could make more money making bricks.

I had been planting and harvesting alongside my grandmother, mother, and neighbors since I recovered from smallpox. We sang as we worked, but while the others looked on with approval at how quickly my small fingers sent seeds into the ground and pulled up vegetables, they shook their heads and covered their ears at my voice. "Eat betel nut," they told me. "That will make you sing better."

I knew that chewing betel nut, the seeds that grow on areca palm trees, would make my teeth black. I'd pre-chewed it before until it was soft enough for Bà Nội, who enjoyed the flavor but had no teeth. Whether it would really help me sing, though, I wasn't sure. I went to a friend whose teeth were always black and asked her to sing. Her voice was as bad as mine, so I decided not to bother with the betel nut. I was still the hardest worker and would continue to sing as I wished.

By the time I was six, I was given the crucial job of keeping the rice paddies wet. This involved long hours of dipping a bucket into a nearby creek, scurrying back across the farm, and pouring the water into the rice paddy. Without enough water, the rice would stop growing and eventually die. Without those paddies, my family might, too.

They were the center of our world, not because we ate much of the tiny white grains—in fact, only rarely did we each get to savor even a precious spoonful. Selling rice at the village market was the main way we bought things we could not grow ourselves. The small, white fish that darted around the rice paddies were a centerpiece of our dinners. On days when both rice and fish ran dry, we gnawed on yuca and malanga from our farm, our bodies faint with hunger.

One afternoon, though, when I was about seven years old, food literally began falling from the sky. Word spread fast: I saw a swarm of children race to a field and return cradling tiny circular metal tins in their skinny arms. I joined the crowd around them. Lucky for me, a boy I knew had collected ten of these tins, and I convinced him to give me just one.

It fit into the palm of my hand. I ran my fingers over the brown label. I didn't recognize the writing on it, but it looked like pieces of cabbage in the picture. I ran home where my family was gathered and immediately pulled back the top. Inside was a murky red mixture with a pungent smell that hung heavy in the air and traveled far. We all peered closer: It looked like a mysterious jungle of chopped cabbage and some kind of pepper. My family took turns taking a deep inhale. Everyone looked disgusted, but not me. I took another deep breath and thought hard about what I smelled. There was a sourness that reminded me of the mustard greens we left out overnight to pickle.

It would be decades before I learned that the can contained the Korean fermented cabbage known as kimchi, and that the supplies were airdropped for South Korean soldiers who had come to Vietnam to support South Vietnamese troops. But in my family's hut that day, we had no idea if the mixture was even edible.

My mother asked, "What are you going to do with this?"

"Do you eat it?" Bà Nội asked.

"Maybe I'll try it, Bà Nội," I answered.

My mother looked horrified. "You can't eat that. You might die!"

I stuck my finger into the sauce, then popped it into my mouth. It didn't taste like much. After rinsing one of the leaf-like pieces and examining it closely, I saw that with its tiny wrinkles, it looked much different than the smooth, round green cabbage we grew. My mother's friend was part of a group of villagers who regularly traveled a day's bus ride south to work in Dalat, a large vegetable-growing area. She recognized it as a variety called napa, a type of Chinese cabbage.

I began to think about what I should do. I went to my mother and asked for a few precious coins so that her friend could bring one of these cabbages back from Dalat. I almost never asked for money—I knew my parents didn't have much—but I was just so curious. My mother said yes, and several days later my very own napa cabbage arrived.

It was so tall! And so strange with its crinkly top! It sat heavy in my hands as I turned it around and around studying its light-green shade. When I cut it in half, I was shocked by its blinding-white middle. The next step was to make a more delicious version of what was in the tin.

My mind went to what we grew on the farm that made everything taste good. Garlic. Ginger. Green onions. Hot red peppers. I pounded those together with a mortar and pestle to form a rough sauce. I chopped the cabbage as widely as I had found it in the tin, using only half of it in case my experiment didn't work. Then I spread the sauce on top and left it out overnight, covered. The next day, I mixed everything together. The cabbage had become soft and fragrant. Family and friends gathered around for a bite. "So good!" they said. "Make more!"

I did the same thing with the other half of the cabbage, and got praise from everyone again. Not long after, my mother's friend brought me a baby napa cabbage, which I planted on our farm. Several months later, we had an entire crop of cabbage that had never before been grown in Điện Bàn.

I was doing many things without an adult. I was farming rice by myself by the time I was eight years old. I later began selling the cabbage, along with our rice and other vegetables, at the market, giving the money to my parents to help pay for school for my four younger brothers. Even though I had decided that school was not for me, I still wanted them to have an education.

+ + +

A few times a year, my grandmother would make special dinners featuring the only meat we ate all year. Those meals left our stomachs satisfied for days. I had watched and helped her enough times to know that I could cook one by myself, and by the age of eight, I knew exactly when I wanted to start: the annual family festival honoring my grandfather, Bà Nội's late husband, on the anniversary of his death. My parents and Bà Nội discussed this possibility and agreed.

My father gave me permission to use two of our chickens that clucked their way around the farm. I knew they were the only chickens we could spare for the festival, and that it might be months before we ate meat again. If I ruined the chickens, I would ruin the entire celebration. I dreaded the look of disappointment that would spread over Bà Nội's face if that happened.

I tried to focus on making the most delicious meal possible, one that would bring a look of pride to Bà Nội's face. First, I prepared stock. I went to the outdoor area we used as a kitchen. It was shaded by an awning of rice-paddy stalks and had a wood-fired stove made of brick and a flat board for cutting. I put all of the chicken, pork, and turkey bones I could afford to buy in a pot with water, then set it on the stove to simmer gently.

Next, I had to butcher the chickens, which I had never done before. All of the adults were off preparing for the festival, so I grabbed one and cut its throat with a knife as I had seen my father do before other special dinners. The chicken began to bleed, but it also continued to squirm. It took several long minutes before the squirming stopped.

I did the same with the other chicken, then ran down to the river to wash both birds. I boiled water, dipped the chicken in it, and pulled off the feathers, mimicking my grandmother. I took out the innards and cut the birds in half, my hands shaking with nerves.

Along with the meaty stock, I decided to assemble two different dishes using some of my grandmother's staple ingredients. One combined chicken with ginger, the other with curry and chunks of sweet potatoes. Soon, the smells from the simmering pots told me I had made something delicious.

When my family returned, I could see Bà Nội smelling the air. She looked into my pots. "Oh, my God," she said even before picking up a spoon and taking a taste. Her face looked as proud as I had hoped for. That night, everyone agreed: From now on, I would be the one cooking for all the family festivals. I heard Bà Nội saying to my mother, "Don't worry about Tung."

After I had cooked alone for five parties, including one for the whole village, Bà Nội pulled me aside. I knew my family approved of my cooking, even if they didn't say it very often. (Vietnamese believe that terrible things might happen to children who are praised too much.)

Bà Nội looked deep into my eyes and told me that I was her most cherished grandchild. "I know you will take care of me," she said.

Then her wrinkled fist stretched open, and I gasped at the sight of a brilliant ruby ring, which gleamed in the sunlight. I had seen only simple gold wedding bands before. I had no idea that something this beautiful could exist. The ring was a gift from my grandfather long ago, my grandmother explained. He had spent hours and hours making clay for road tiles, saving a little money here and there, to buy Bà Nội this piece of jewelry that shone more brightly than any other.

Bà Nội put the ring in my hand. I slipped it on, and my finger disappeared behind the huge stone. "I'm giving this to you," she said. "Never sell it."

It was the easiest promise I had ever made.

Curried Chicken and Sweet Potatoes

This is the Hy Vong version of the dish Tung learned to make with her grandmother. After experimenting for years, she decided that she prefers it with heavy cream instead of the traditional coconut milk. You can use coconut milk if you like, but it curdles when you add it to a hot curry. So first cool the curry until it's lukewarm (about 30 minutes), then add the coconut milk before gently reheating the curry.

SERVES 4

One 4 to 5 lb [1.8 to 2.3 kg] chicken, cut into 10 pieces (each breast should be halved crosswise), wing tips removed

⅓ cup [80 ml] vegetable oil

1 small sweet onion, chopped

1 Tbsp curry powder

3 large sweet potatoes, peeled and cut crosswise into thirds

1 small stalk of lemongrass, white part only, thinly sliced (discard tough outer layers)

¼ cup [60 ml] fish sauce

1 tsp kosher salt

½ tsp black pepper

6½ cups [1.5 L] Hy Vong Stock (page 66), hot or warm

½ cup [120 ml] heavy cream or coconut milk (see headnote)

4 cups [480 g] cooked jasmine rice, for serving

3 green onions, sliced, for garnish

½ cup [20 g] chopped cilantro leaves, for garnish

Remove any large pieces of fat from the chicken, then rinse the chicken in a strainer. While it drains, heat the oil in large pot over medium heat. Lower the heat to low and add half of the chopped onion, then cook until soft and translucent, about 5 minutes. Stir in the curry powder, then add the chicken, remaining onion, the sweet potato, lemongrass, fish sauce, salt, pepper, and stock. Stir to combine.

Cover the pot and bring to boil over high heat. Lower the heat and simmer, stirring occasionally, until the potato is just tender but not mushy and the chicken is cooked through, 25 to 30 minutes.

Remove from the heat and stir in the heavy cream. If using coconut milk, cool the curry until lukewarm before adding it, then gently reheat the curry. Serve over rice and garnish with the scallions and cilantro.

Hy Vong Stock

This stock plays a key role in many of Hy Vong's most beloved and flavorful dishes, including Curried Chicken and Sweet Potatoes (page 64), Pumpkin Soup (Bí Đỏ) with Fried Shallots (page 27), and Spicy Ribs (Thịt Sườn; page 209). It's worth making a large batch and freezing any extra for future use.

MAKES ABOUT 5 QT [4.7 L]

4 lb [1.8 kg] chicken backs, necks, or feet, or any raw chicken bones with the meat scraped off, large pieces of fat trimmed

3 lb [1.4 kg] beef short ribs or beef neck or soup bones (or 1½ lb plus 1½ lb cow's feet)

2 lb [910 g] pork neck or back or any other pork bones

2 lb [910 g] turkey wings or legs

Rinse the chicken backs, short ribs, pork bones, and turkey under cold running water, removing any bone fragments. In a large pot, combine the bones and 6 qt [5.7 L] of cold water and bring to a boil over high heat. Skim any scum off the surface and stir. Lower the heat and gently simmer for 1 hour, occasionally skimming any scum, stirring, and skimming again.

Stop skimming and stirring, and continue to gently simmer for 2 hours more. Resist the urge to raise the heat; this may make the stock cloudy. Turn off the heat and let the stock sit for 10 to 15 minutes so the fat can rise to the top. Skim any fat, then strain the stock through a large fine-mesh strainer. You should have 4½ to 5½ qt [4.3 to 5.2 L] of stock. If necessary, add water to reach 4½ qt [4.3 L], or continue to simmer if you have more than 5½ qt [5.2 L]. Use the stock immediately, or cool and transfer to airtight containers. Refrigerate for up to 3 days or freeze for up to 3 months.

CHAPTER 6

The General

Iowa and Miami, 1944 to 1975

KATHY:

From my perch high in the maple tree, I could see a car driving back and forth in front of my house. It was a boy—yet another boy hoping that my teenage sister Kris would come outside. I pushed the branches apart so I could see the car clearly.

Its windows were wide open. A clear target. I gripped the garden hose I'd pulled up the tree with me and strained my head to catch the eye of my friend Becky, who was next to the outdoor faucet. "Now!" I yelled.

Becky turned the knob, and I aimed the hose right into the driver's-side window. It was a perfect shot! The target was drenched and more than a little stunned. We didn't see him again for a while, but there was always someone else to have fun with.

I had appointed myself "The General" of our small town, Ames, which was about thirteen blocks wide and lined with cherry and apple trees. I corralled boys and girls to join my army. We marched down the streets, lifting our legs in unison, pretending we were soldiers practicing military drills. Sometimes we marched a block to our elementary school and performed our drills on the playground.

When I wasn't giving orders, I was defying them. Sometimes I took a bus to Iowa State's veterinary school fifteen minutes away and hopped the barbed-wire fence to ride the horses in the field. I didn't bother asking permission or using a saddle: I just jumped onto their bare backs and let them take me wherever they wanted. I liked hanging on tight, not knowing where they would wander. The fact that the horses shared a field with bulls didn't faze me a bit—until one day, when I was about to mount a horse, a bull charged at me. I raced back to the fence, yanked myself over the wire, and was rewarded with a big gash in my stomach. I tried to treat it myself because I knew I would get in trouble if I told my mother what had happened. When the cut became infected, I had to tell my parents anyway. I didn't get punished, but I did get a lifelong scar.

Both of my parents grew up in Ames. My father worked as a gas engineer, traveling frequently for work. My mother mostly stayed home with their five children. We kids never traveled, except to nearby states. I loved living in a house where lots of people were always around, and having big sleepover parties, especially when my father had to step over lines of bodies lying on the floor when he came home late from work. I most loved big family dinners with all my squabbling siblings around the table.

While we always had plenty to eat, my mother had not inherited Grandma Peterson's joy when it came to cooking. She rarely made anything from scratch, relying on mixes and cans. But around holiday time, she could always be found stirring a large pot of her luscious homemade vanilla sauce. It was easy to assemble and could be poured over any dessert—pies, cakes, bread pudding—to make it more special.

Motherhood overwhelmed my mother. I was daughter number four, the last one, and by the time my mother got to me, she was tired and forgot to teach me all the social graces and manners that my sisters seemed to know. She just let me grow up wild, like a weed. One day she handed me silver dog tags embossed with my name and address. "I can't stop you from running all over town, but I can make sure that you get home," she said.

As my friends and I grew older, they became interested in boy-girl parties, clothes, and makeup, just like my sisters. I preferred taking apart our family's only radio or my mother's car to look at the wires and mechanics—or playing softball, baseball, or ice hockey, all of which my mother considered unladylike. I did try going to school dances once or twice, but no one wanted to dance with me.

I often felt removed from what everyone else my age was doing, and it was tough for me to connect with them, even though I wanted to. To get around this, I learned to joke a lot and became the class clown: Making jokes gave me an excuse to talk to people.

The only place I felt truly comfortable was at Grandma Peterson's. She lived a few streets away, and I started spending more time there than at home. Grandma could tell that my relentless energy needed an outlet, so she put me to work. I helped her hand-wash the laundry and hang it in the backyard and paint houses that she bought to fix up to rent or sell.

I also started working for others. I mowed just about every small yard in town, delivered the *Ames Tribune* on my bike, stacked the grocery store shelves with Wonder Bread, shoveled snow, and sold night crawler worms for fishing.

One of the best parts of being at Grandma's house was spending time with her foster children. She took in two or three at a time. Most of them came from homes filled with abuse and arrived with just a few garments in a small tattered bag. In addition to food, clothing, and shelter, Grandma gave them unconditional love and a strict routine of school, playtime, dinner, bath, and bed.

I could see them get calmer during their stays, and they always left both physically stronger and happier. She gave them a parting gift of clothes and a teddy bear or other comfort object.

Grandma never viewed being a foster parent as a burden; to her, it was simply part of being a Christian and person who helped others. She told me she loved how children were alive and open, whereas adults her age "just complained."

"Give me the children," she quipped. "Don't put me with the old folks."

+ + +

When I was sixteen, my parents announced that we were moving to Miami. My father had accepted a new job. Miami? It might as well have been the moon. My entire world was Ames and Iowa. I had never even been on a plane.

We left our home in September 1960. Miami was everything Iowa wasn't. Humid. Loud. Full of pink houses and palm trees. A few days after we arrived, Hurricane Donna blew in, knocking down trees, flooding streets, and stranding us in our hotel. I disregarded the warnings and tiptoed outside in the eye of the storm. It was eerily quiet.

After the hurricane ended, I tried to get my head around Miami. I stood on the beach and, for the first time, looked at the rolling ocean—so different from the waving cornfields of Iowa. I saw Latin restaurants and heard Spanish spoken everywhere. I gawked at the pink churches and store displays of fresh fish and new-to-me fruits like papaya and mango. I was used to a diet of meat and potatoes and had never eaten fish that hadn't been frozen first. Unlike small-town Ames, Miami seemed to sprawl out forever. It was too much for me. I missed home. I did not belong in Florida, and I decided to do something about it.

Once school started, I began saving my lunch money. When I had enough for bus fare back to Iowa, I left a note for my parents telling them I was leaving, then walked out the door and boarded a bus.

I didn't make it far. My parents found the note sooner than I expected and called the police, who were waiting for me when the bus stopped at the West Palm Beach station. At least my parents got the message that I was unhappy. They let me go back to Iowa alone for a visit during Christmas vacation. I was happy to see Grandma Peterson, but I missed my parents and my siblings. I grudgingly accepted that Miami was where I lived now. There was no use resisting it. I needed to put down roots.

To my delight, I found more opportunities in Miami as a woman who enjoyed sports. I joined the softball, volleyball, badminton, and basketball teams at my high school and became president of the athletic club. My senior year, I was voted Outstanding Woman Athlete. On the non-sports side, I won a writing award from the *Miami Herald* for an essay on citizenship, joined a church, became president of the Lutheran club, and made some good friends along the way.

After graduating in 1963, I enrolled in Dade County Community College (now Miami-Dade Community College), but after one year, I decided I wanted to travel instead. Living in Miami had made me realize there was a whole world out there to explore. I wanted to see how other people lived and to help others—and I wanted to do those things right away.

I decided to move to New York City, specifically Harlem. President Lyndon B. Johnson's Neighborhood Youth Corps was recruiting people to assist local children with finding jobs, so I applied and was hired. I loved working with the kids. They inspired me with their energy, enthusiasm, and hopes for a better future. I could see that they loved to dream, but they had no idea how to dream beyond what they saw.

It was easy to be disillusioned by the problems in Harlem. I was trying to break barriers so that people would have more opportunity, but I found that my superiors didn't always agree. I was dismayed when they used proceeds from a coffeehouse that I ran for them to build a fence around the local church instead of using the money to educate people or build spaces that would bring us all together. I thought we were working to build community, not put up barriers.

After a year of diligently saving, I had enough money to fulfill my dream of backpacking around Europe for a year. I started my trip in colorful Barcelona. From there, I was excited to travel to my family's native Sweden but didn't stay long. Its culture was so proper and buttoned-up, I felt stifled. When I got to Italy, I felt much more at home. The loud, joyous, freewheeling, wine-drinking culture suited me perfectly. I studied German in Munich. I bought a motor scooter and was planning to go through the Alps in the dead of winter back to Italy, but it broke down outside of Munich— this, in retrospect, probably saved my life. I was planning to head to Israel to work on a kibbutz when I realized I had run out of money, so I returned to Miami to live with my parents.

There, I enrolled at Barry University to finish my bachelor's degree and got a waitressing job at a local restaurant. I enjoyed serving people and truly thought that I could help others by being a waitress as much as I could by being a social worker. That view was not shared by any of my coworkers, who just counted their money and spent all the time they could smoking out back. They didn't care about service. It put a real damper on my enthusiasm, and I declared to myself more than once, "When I finish university, I am never going to work in another restaurant!"

I rode everywhere in Miami on a motor scooter, which was cheaper than buying a car. One day, my helmet had been stolen while I was at work. I had no other way to get home, so I rode without a helmet, taking my usual route through what was then a predominantly African-American neighborhood. Five blocks from home, I got pulled over by a policeman.

"What do you mean, going this way?" he asked me.

I assumed the officer was a redneck, telling me I should avoid the area for racist reasons. "That's the way I go, and that's the way I will continue to go," I responded.

"You don't have a helmet," he said.

"It was stolen," I replied.

He gave me a ticket, took my license, and followed me to make sure I got home safely. Later, I learned there had been a riot in the neighborhood I'd just driven through. The policeman didn't tell me that—if he had, we would have understood each other a little better. We had just made assumptions without really communicating.

I went to court to get my license back. I explained to the judge that I had no choice but to drive home without a helmet.

"Sir, I didn't do this wantonly," I said. "My helmet was stolen. I don't think it's fair that I pay a fine."

The judge was baffled. "You mean you'd rather go to jail than pay a fine?"

"Yes, sir," I said.

"Okay," the judge replied. "Five days."

"I think I have the right to appeal," I told the bailiff as he escorted me out. He told me no.

I called my mother to let her know what had happened, then I sat in jail overnight. It was uncomfortable, but I didn't regret my decision: I knew I was right. While I was there, my brother called the judge and successfully asked for me to be freed early. (Years later, the judge ate at our restaurant, and we became friends without initially knowing who the other person was.)

When I finally graduated from Barry University at twenty-eight, having taken several breaks from school to work and travel, many people my age were in serious relationships or already married. I was attracted to men, but settling down with someone had never been a priority for me, or even something that I was interested in. I wanted to do what I wanted to do when I wanted to do it. I wanted to be free and unencumbered.

While thinking about my future, I realized that social work was not for me after all—the government regulations were too constraining. So, I decided to go back to school to get my teaching degree. I knew I loved being around kids, wanted to help others, and enjoyed showing people how to do things. I also liked being able to problem-solve using my own ideas and methods. My friends always joked: "Don't tell her how to do it, just give her a hint."

Like Grandma Peterson, I wanted to work with people who needed me, and I wanted to make them happy. I wanted to help them dream as big as I did. And I wanted to do all of this while being true to myself.

Bread Pudding with Vanilla Sauce

One of Kathy's favorite childhood comfort foods was the vanilla sauce made by her mother, Gwendolyn Manning. Later, Kathy found a way for Hy Vong's customers to enjoy it, too: She used it over this bread pudding, resulting in one of the restaurant's most popular desserts. Feel free to add more raisins, if you like.

SERVES 12 TO 16

24 slices butter crust sandwich bread, such as Sara Lee Butter Bread (about 1⅓ loaves), no end pieces

1½ cups [330 g] unsalted butter, at room temperature (preferably Plugrá or another European-style butter)

1½ cups [210 g] golden raisins

¾ cup [150 g] sugar

½ tsp cinnamon

Four 12 oz [360 ml] cans evaporated milk

½ tsp kosher salt

3 large eggs

1 tsp vanilla extract

Vanilla Sauce (page 77), for serving

Preheat the broiler on high and set a rack about 6 in [15 cm] below the heating element. Generously butter a 9 by 13 in [23 by 33 cm] baking dish and set it on a larger baking sheet to catch any drips.

On a large baking sheet or broiler pan, broil 6 slices of the bread on one side until lightly toasted, about 30 seconds. (You can also toast the slices individually in a toaster.) Thickly butter each slice on the broiled side. Cut each slice in half and arrange them in a single layer in the baking dish, buttered-side up. The dish should fit 12 halves in a single layer. Sprinkle about one-fourth of the raisins on top.

continued

Repeat with the next 6 slices of bread, alternating the direction the slices are facing in the dish. Sprinkle another one-fourth of the raisins on top. Repeat with the remaining bread, butter, and raisins, alternating the direction the slices are facing.

Turn off the broiler and preheat the oven to 350°F [180°C], with a rack in the middle position.

Meanwhile, in a small bowl, combine ¼ cup [50 g] of the sugar and the cinnamon. Set aside.

In a medium pot, combine the milk, 1 cup [240 ml] of water, the remaining ½ cup [100 g] of sugar, and the salt. Place over high heat, stirring occasionally, for 3 minutes. In a separate bowl, lightly beat the eggs. After the milk mixture has warmed for 3 minutes, scoop out about 1 cup and gradually whisk it into the eggs. Let the remaining milk mixture come to a simmer, without stirring. Gradually add the egg-milk mixture to the pot, whisking constantly, until thoroughly combined. Bring to a gentle simmer, then remove from the heat and stir in the vanilla.

Pour the custard over the bread a little at a time, simultaneously using a fork to prick holes in the bread and gently pull the bread away from the sides of the pan, allowing the custard to reach all the nooks and crannies. Let sit for about 15 minutes so the bread can absorb the milk. Sprinkle the cinnamon sugar over the top and bake, uncovered, until a knife inserted into the center comes out clean, about 40 minutes. Serve warm, topped with warm vanilla sauce.

Vanilla Sauce

At Hy Vong, we served this sauce warm over our Bread
Pudding (page 75). It's also good warm or cold on pies and
cakes, or over berries. The sauce thickens as it cools, giving
it a more luscious consistency.

MAKES ABOUT 4½ CUPS [1 L]

3 cups [720 ml] heavy cream

1½ cups [300 g] sugar

¾ cup [165 g] unsalted butter

3 Tbsp cornstarch

1 Tbsp vanilla extract

In a medium heavy saucepan, combine the cream, sugar, and
butter and cook over medium heat, stirring occasionally, until
the butter melts, the sugar dissolves, and the mixture starts
to boil.

Meanwhile, in a small bowl, stir together ½ cup [120 ml] of
cold water and the cornstarch. When the cream mixture boils,
whisk in the cornstarch mixture. Continue cooking, whisking
constantly until the mixture is thick enough to coat the back
of a spoon, 1 to 2 minutes more. Remove from the heat and
gently stir in the vanilla. The sauce can be used immediately
or after it cools. It will keep, in an airtight container, in the
refrigerator for up to 5 days.

CHAPTER 7

Selling Soup

Vietnam, 1957 to 1975

TUNG:

People from my village never dreamed of traveling around the world. Or having a big, fancy house with lots of rooms. Or going to a college. We knew all that would never happen.

What did we dream about? Growing perfect grains of rice. Or recovering from smallpox. Or cooking plentiful meals for the whole village. We also knew all that would take a long time. We had a saying, "Kiến tha lâu cũng đầy tổ." It meant "ants gather food day by day to fill their nest." If we saved little by little and worked hard each day, then we would reach our goals in time.

I had allowed myself one huge dream since I was a child: that my mother and father could live in a brick house.

Everyone in Điện Bàn lived in a house made of either brick or stalks from the rice paddies. If you lived in the first type, you had status. People in the village treated you with respect.

You could also sit in your house without fear of rain coming through the roof and sleep without hearing the wind whistle through the walls.

If you lived in the second type, like my family did, you were always treated poorly by those who lived in brick houses. You also constantly had to paste over the holes that developed in the structure. That involved gathering oyster shells, crushing each one, turning that into a paste, then spreading it on the outside of the house where needed. The worst part was, you knew the paste would last for only so long before you had to do it all over again.

When I was a teenager, I became determined to build my parents a brick house. What would I need? Money. Bricks. Help. Time. I had none of those, but that had never stopped me before. I approached my grandmother: "Bà Nội, I know what to do. You must keep it a secret. You must not tell my mother and father. I am going to make my own bricks!"

"Really?" Bà Nội asked. "How? Do you know how to make bricks?"

"No," I said. "I have to learn."

After the rice-farming season ended and I had more time, I went to the brickmaker's shop, where my father worked. I told him that I wanted to learn brickmaking, but I did not say why.

"The work is too heavy for you," my father said.

Later, at home, my mother agreed with him, adding, "You're too young."

So I waited until no one was watching and snuck off in secret whenever I could, avoiding the areas where my father worked. I spent hours there watching the many steps needed to make a single brick: stripping the top soil to unearth the gray dirt underneath; stomping and turning it until it became clay; kneading fistfuls of clay and throwing them as hard as possible into molds so that they would spread into all the corners; leveling off the bricks and leaving them to dry for two days; baking them in the oven for several days; then finally cooling them for several days. Each part of the process had to be carried out just right, or the brick would not be useable.

After several months, I had watched enough brickmaking that I knew I could do it myself. Now, I needed to get a job at the shop. I approached my father again and was relieved when he gave his okay this time, even though he still didn't know my real plan. I went to the head brickmaker and told him if he hired me, he didn't have to pay me as much as everyone else. I just wanted to keep some of the bricks I made until I had enough to build a one-room house for my parents.

After getting over his surprise, the boss said I could have one brick out of every ten that I made, and that it would take about six months to meet my goal. I was so happy, and got right to work. Because I had spent so much time watching what to do, I made bricks much better and faster than anyone expected. Each night, I piled up to thirty bricks on a makeshift wagon and rolled them home. As the pile outside my parents' house grew larger, and they grew more suspicious, I told them I knew someone who would buy them from me. They weren't totally convinced.

"Why is Tung keeping so many bricks?" my father asked Bà Nội.

"I don't know," she lied.

After only three months, the pile had grown high enough to build the house. I gathered my entire family outside and pointed at the bricks. "I will not be selling these bricks," I said. "I will be building a house for mother and father." Next, I presented my parents with the earnings from my job—enough money to pay people in the village to help build the house.

My mother wept. My father teared up, then walked away so that others would not see him cry. When he returned, he said, "I don't need to eat dinner. I am full of happiness."

We built the house, except for the roof, in ten days, paying some people in food cooked by my mother and Bà Nội. I glowed with pride as I saw the men grinding up oyster shells and mixing them into a paste—not to smear over rice-paddy stalks, but to glue the bricks together to form solid walls.

After the walls were finished, we had to build the roof before we could move in. That involved me working at the clay tile shop. It took a whole year to earn enough tiles for the roof, but at last, my parents had the house I'd always dreamed of. It was always dry inside, and no one could treat us poorly again for living in a house made of rice-paddy stalks.

A year later, Bà Nội passed away. My world went black as I tried to adjust to life without my grandmother. I took comfort in gazing at the tight rows of brick in my parents' home. Each time, I affectionately recalled our secret, and saw her toothless smile of approval.

+ + +

When I was twenty-two, my father started saying that his head hurt. I ran across the village to find my uncle, who was an expert in Chinese herbal medicine—the only medicine we knew. The herbs he gave me didn't stop my father's pain, so I went to another expert, who recommended the same herbs. I then cooked him rice soup, which I thought might help, but that didn't work either.

As I thought about what else to do, my father went to sleep. He never woke up. My mother knelt over his body, silently cradling her growing stomach. This would be her seventh child. "Your father left me too many children," she said. "Now what do I do?"

"Don't worry," I replied. "Leave it to me."

I knew that because I was a girl, everyone thought that supporting my family would be too much for me. But there was no one else. My next-oldest sibling, my brother Mau, was the one who lost his eyesight from smallpox, and most people considered him non-existent. The responsibility sank into me alongside waves of grief.

I went to buy a coffin for my father. I selected a simple wooden box with unsanded planks. Although I longed to get a

81

nicer one, working to pay for that would put me behind in harvesting rice. And I needed that rice to feed my family.

When the Buddhist monk arrived the next day to lead the procession to the grave, I could not accept that my father was gone. I asked my mother to do one thing for me at the burial. In Vietnam, sand is tossed onto a grave to symbolize that the dead person has returned to the earth. My mother could throw her own sand onto my father's grave from her right hand, as we commonly did at funerals. Then she would also throw sand from her left hand for me.

After everyone left, the house was so quiet. In the silence, I could feel my father's spirit. He told me to keep working, keep thinking. I would lead my family. I would be enough. I cried long and loudly.

Later, one of my uncles approached my mother with an offer that he said would help all of us. He would take my two youngest brothers. They could help him with his farming, and that would be two fewer children in our house to feed, clothe, and educate.

I knew Kiem and Nhut would be treated like slaves. "My brothers, you leave to me!" I yelled. I told my mother to pay him no attention.

I worked as much as I could—farming, making more bricks, whatever I could do—but I just couldn't bring in the money my family needed. Then I had an idea. Sometimes a few ladies would sell bún bò huế on a street not far from my village. People bought the beef noodle soup for four dong a bowl. If I sold several bowls a day, that kind of money would be a small fortune to my family.

"I want to sell soup," I told my mother. "Bún bò."

"You know how to cook bún bò?" she answered.

"I have to learn."

+ + +

I was already the best soup maker in our village. People came to me for tips on how to make phở, pumpkin soup, duck and rice soup . . .

I knew which bones made the best broth. I knew exactly how long to simmer them, when to skim the scum off the top, and when to just leave them alone. However, I had never made or even eaten bún bò huế, even though it was the specialty soup of our region. I walked until I found a bún bò vendor. I gave her money and she handed me a steaming bowl filled with a dark broth and topped with a tangle of fresh green herbs.

"What is in it?" I asked.

"Pig's feet, beef, noodles, onion, lemongrass," she replied.

I sat down and ate it, concentrating on the flavors. I thought about the combination of meat and spice and tartness. It was good, but I could make it better.

My mother and I harvested more rice, yuca, and malanga to take to the village market to trade for the beef and pork bones needed to make the soup. We also sold the last of our tobacco leaf and chickens in order to buy ten bowls and pairs of chopsticks for serving my eventual customers. When we got home, I covered the bones in water in the biggest pot we had and let them slowly simmer over the fire for several hours. Meanwhile, I assembled the rest of the things I'd need to carry and sell my soup, including a long bamboo pole with baskets hanging from shorter sticks at either end and a small portable clay stove.

It took some experimenting, but once I got the broth right, it was easy to figure out the rest of the soup. I prepped enough of everything, loaded up the baskets, squatted so I could center the long pole across my shoulders, and stood up, ready to walk the 2 miles [3.2 km] to the main road that led to Đà Nẵng. I knew that was where I could find the most people willing to pay for the soup.

Once there, I found a man with a cigarette lighter and asked him to light the wood in my stove. I placed my pot on top to keep the broth hot and was ready for business. At my side was the serving spoon that my father had made years ago out of a stick and halved coconut shell. For the next few hours, I served customer after customer, all the while hearing noises of approval.

"Oh, my God!" "What is in this?" "So good!"

I went home with enough money to buy food for my family, to make the next payment to my siblings' school, and to make my mother weep with gratitude.

Now I had a way to keep my family together and buy everything we needed. Seven days a week, I rose before the sun, made one pot of broth; prepared piles of herbs, onion, beef, and noodles; then started a second pot of broth, which my mother tended while I headed to my selling spot. Before long, I would arrive to find customers already waiting for me, even when I returned with the second batch of broth later in the day. I raised my price to five dong and still sold out of both batches daily: a total of several dozen bowls of bún bò huế. By the time I walked home—my fourth 2 mile [3.2 km] trip of the day—it was usually getting dark.

My soup continued to sell out, so I kept raising my prices. Over the next couple of years, I raised it to six, then seven, and then eight dong. I carried so much cash on my trips between my selling spot and home that my mother feared someone would attack me. It made a huge difference in our lives. For the first time my siblings had real shoes, not just feet covers made out of tree bark like I wore. My mother wanted to buy me a pair, too, but I shook my head. I had everything I needed now that my family was taken care of and happy.

+ + +

By the end of year three, though, fewer and fewer people were buying my soup, and I wasn't sure why. I went down to making one pot a day, and eventually began spending less time selling soup and more time working on our farm alongside Sinh, my childhood friend.

I liked Sinh. She was as hard a worker as I was; quiet and gentle, too. She also listened to all my ideas of what to do now that I couldn't rely on my income selling soup. I knew she understood how much I needed money, as her family was just as poor. I told her that the word *Saigon* kept popping in my head. I had heard my customers talking about it. It was a big city, a beautiful city, they said. And people there loved to eat soup.

"Sinh," I said, "maybe you and I should go to Saigon." It was so far, such a big risk. I could never do it alone. But maybe I could do it with Sinh. She could run soup to customers while I prepared the broth. Or the opposite. Most important, if anything ever happened to me, Sinh could get word back to my mother.

She looked terrified when I brought up the subject, but I assured her that we would be fine and make lots of money to help our families. If I admitted how scared I was, I knew Sinh would not go with me.

"Will your parents give you permission to go?" I asked. Because we were single, our culture dictated that we had to get their approval. Because my father was dead, I had to get permission first from my mother, then from one of my uncles. Sinh went home and asked. Her mother thought it was a good idea; her father wasn't sure. My mother felt the same as her father. We all met for lunch at my mother's house to talk over the big idea.

"Do you know how to get to Saigon?" my mother asked us.

"I don't, but Tung does," Sinh answered.

In fact, I didn't. I just assumed I could find out. I had heard from customers that there was a bus and a train. I told our families what a great opportunity it could be for everyone, especially compared to our options at home. Eventually, all the parents nodded. My uncle agreed, too.

I packed up a few clothes and my big soup pot. My mother had been keeping my grandmother's ring safe for me over the years but knew I'd want to have it with me as I traveled to this new city. She brought it out of its hiding place and helped me tuck it into a small pocket inside my pants. We fastened a little hook to the pocket so that it would stay closed.

I was twenty-six on my last night in Điện Bàn. I cooked dinner for our families and friends. Everyone crowded around to say goodbye to Sinh and me, the girls who were headed to Saigon. Not a single person from the village had ever been there.

+ + +

Early the next morning, Sinh and I walked to the main road that led to Đà Nẵng. Right away, we bumped into one of my customers. "Why are you not selling bún bò?" he asked.

"We are going to Saigon," I replied. "I can make more money there. Do you know how we get there?"

He pointed us down the road to Đà Nẵng and told us there was a train, but that it was very expensive. "Take the bus," he said. "It will take two days, but it is much cheaper."

Sinh and I found the station, figured out how to buy our tickets, and crammed onto the next bus. It was my first ride in a vehicle, and it moved faster than I had ever moved before. The ride was so bumpy! Sinh and I watched the landscape change through the windows. We saw trees filled with bananas, jackfruit, and mangoes. We saw so many birds, especially in the morning. We passed sugarcane plantations and rubber plantations and noticed how much fancier the homes looked the closer we got to the city.

"Why are you so quiet, Chị Hai?" Sinh asked me as we approached Saigon. She had started calling me that. It meant "oldest sister" and was a sign of respect.

"I'm nervous," I finally admitted.

Sinh's eyes widened. "Oh, my God," she said. "Why didn't you tell me that before?"

"If I told you before, you would have stayed home!" I said. "And then I couldn't go. I couldn't do this myself."

Sinh didn't say anything back.

When we pulled into the station, we were tired, scared, nauseated from the ride, and sticky from the heat. The buildings around us were so big, and everything looked different. We asked a rickshaw driver to take us to the closest market, and he drove us to Chợ Bến Thành, the large indoor market in the heart of the city near the Saigon River. There we found a cheap room with a kitchen to rent and an open area with a table and chairs right outside of it—the perfect place to live and sell soup.

Quickly, we settled into a routine. Early each morning, I made the broth while Sinh prepared the other ingredients, and then we spent the day selling the soup. We never took a day off. Eventually I learned of a butcher across town who sold soup bones much more cheaply than at the market. So I started getting up at four in the morning for a thirty-five-minute rickshaw ride to pick them up. I also started using more bones and different types, such as turkey wings and marrowbones, to create the richest, most flavorful broth in the market. Once the butcher knew my standing order, he placed all of my bones and meat in a bamboo bucket that was waiting for me when I arrived.

From the start, we had so many customers that we had time only to take their orders, and no time to talk to them or anyone else. A year went by in a blur. Our entire world was our soup stand, the butcher, the room in which we slept, and each other. I was so grateful that Sinh had come with me to Saigon. She always knew what I needed, and what we needed to run our stand, without us having to discuss it. She was also a buffer from the wealthy patrons at the market who were constantly insulting us with clever words. They may have liked our soup, but not the fact that we were poor country people.

We didn't know much about the war in Vietnam or how much it was intensifying. We had not seen any violence. Its only impact on us was occasionally serving American and Vietnamese soldiers at our soup stand. I showed one American soldier how to hold chopsticks.

As the spring of 1975 approached, we began planning a visit home the following year to celebrate Tết, the Vietnamese New Year. We hadn't seen our families since we left, though we felt connected to them through the money we sent home every month through one of my uncles, who would travel to Saigon to pick it up.

And there was my grandmother's ring, which I looked at every night before going to bed. That ring drew me closer to the spirit of Bà Nội. It gave me strength. It made me feel like I had the courage to face anything that was ahead of me.

Hearty Beef Noodle Soup (Bún Bò Huế)

Bún bò is the classic soup from Huế, which is near Tung's hometown in central Vietnam. It's not as common in the United States as phở, but it certainly deserves to be: It's the perfect balance of spice, acidity, and deep meatiness. Bún bò huế seasoning is a combination of paprika, chili powder, onion, ginger, and garlic. The brand we recommend is Trong Food International; their label reads Kim Tư Tháp Pyramide Gia Vị Bún Bò Huế. You can find it in Asian grocery stores or online. Pig's and cow's feet and tripe are traditional additions to this soup, but feel free to omit them. The stock, feet, and tripe can be prepared in advance and refrigerated for up to 3 days; the stock can be stored in the freezer for up to 3 months.

SERVES 8

STOCK

3½ to 4 lb [1.6 to 1.8 kg] boneless beef knuckle,
top or bottom round, or sirloin, fat trimmed

2½ lb [1.2 kg] beef marrowbones or short ribs, oxtail,
or any beef soup bones

1½ lb [680 g] turkey wings or legs

1½ lb [680 g] pork neck or other pork bones,
or substitute more beef soup bones

FEET (OPTIONAL)

1½ lb [680 g] pig's feet, cut into about 1 in [2.5 cm] wide
cylinders by a butcher

1¼ lb [570 g] cow's feet, cut into about 1 in [2.5 cm] wide
cylinders by a butcher

TRIPE (OPTIONAL)

1½ lb [680 g] tripe

continued

89

SOUP

1 medium sweet onion, chopped, plus ½ medium sweet onion, halved lengthwise and thinly sliced crosswise, for garnish

1 stalk of lemongrass, white part only, minced (discard tough outer layers)

3 large garlic cloves, minced

1 cup [240 ml] fish sauce

¼ cup [50 g] sugar

2 Tbsp kosher salt

1¼ lb [570 g] thick rice vermicelli (the package will be labeled "Bún Bò Huế noodles")

¼ cup [60 ml] vegetable oil

1 Tbsp bún bò huế seasoning

1 lb [455 g] bean sprouts, crushed lightly with your hands, for garnish

1 bunch green onions, sliced, for garnish

1 cup [40 g] chopped cilantro, leaves and stems, for garnish

8 fresh bird's-eye chiles, sliced, for garnish

2 limes, each cut into 8 wedges, for garnish (optional)

TO MAKE THE STOCK:

Rinse the beef knuckle, beef marrowbones, turkey wings, and pork bones under cold running water, removing any bone fragments. In a large pot, combine them with 8 qt [7.5 L] of water and bring to a boil over high heat. Skim any scum off the surface and stir. Boil for 3 minutes more, then skim and stir again. Lower the heat and gently simmer, occasionally skimming and stirring, for about 2 hours.

Remove the beef knuckle and set aside to cool. Ideally, chill the knuckle until cold; this will make it easier to slice. Cut the meat into four long pieces with the grain, then thinly slice each piece against the grain. If you're making the stock in advance, tightly cover the knuckle and refrigerate for up to 2 days.

Gently simmer the stock, without mixing or skimming, for 1½ hours more. Resist the urge to raise the heat; this will make the stock cloudy. Let sit for 10 to 15 minutes so the fat can rise to the top. Skim any fat and scum off the surface, then strain the stock through a large fine-mesh strainer. You should have 6 to 7 qt [5.7 to 6.6 L] of stock. If necessary, add water to reach 6 qt [5.7 L], or continue to simmer if you have more than 7 qt [6.6 L]. Use the stock immediately, or cool and transfer to airtight containers. Refrigerate for up to 3 days or freeze for up to 3 months.

TO MAKE THE FEET (IF USING):

In a medium saucepan, cover the pig's and cow's feet with cold water and bring to a boil over high heat. Skim any scum off the surface, stir, then lower the heat and simmer until the feet are cooked, about 1½ hours. Drain, then set the feet aside. If you're doing this step in advance, cover the feet with water and refrigerate for up to 2 days.

TO MAKE THE TRIPE (IF USING):

In a medium saucepan, cover the tripe with cold water and bring to a boil over high heat. Lower the heat and simmer until tender, about 20 minutes. Drain, cut the tripe into ½ in [12 mm] slices, and set aside. If you're doing this step in advance, tightly cover the tripe and refrigerate for up to 2 days.

TO MAKE THE SOUP:

In a large pot, combine the stock, beef knuckle meat, pig and cow's feet (if using), tripe (if using), chopped sweet onion, lemongrass, garlic, fish sauce, sugar, and salt and bring to a boil over high heat. As soon as the soup base comes to a boil, remove from the heat.

continued

Meanwhile, prepare the vermicelli according to the package directions. Also, in a small skillet, heat the oil over medium heat. Add the bún bò huế seasoning and stir for about 1 minute to bloom the spices. Stir the mixture into the soup.

To serve, divide the vermicelli among eight deep bowls, followed by the beef knuckle meat, pig and cow's feet (if using), and tripe (if using). Ladle 2 to 3 cups [480 to 720 ml] of the soup base among the bowls and garnish with the sliced sweet onion, bean sprouts, green onions, cilantro, chiles (if using), and lime.

CHAPTER 8

Vietnamese Hot Dogs

Miami, 1975 to 1980

TUNG:

I did not want to yell at Kathy, but I had to. She had brought home a bunch of plastic objects with soft tops—"bottles," she called them. She wanted me to fill them with powdered milk and feed them to my baby. She told me that the milk from my body was not enough. She said Phuong Lien was not getting enough food! Kathy never had a baby. What did she know?

In Vietnam, we did everything naturally. Once Phuong Lien was old enough to eat something besides my milk, I figured I would put food in my mouth, chew it, then feed it to her. That was what I had done for Bà Nội, who had no teeth, and that was what we had always done for babies. But Kathy came home with jars of food that was already ground up. I just left them on the counter. I wanted to cook my own food for my baby. I could make dishes that were more delicious, such as chicken soup with rice or stewed carrots.

Then, when I talked about sewing some clothes, she brought home drawings she called "patterns." Why did I need those? I just got some fabric and a needle and thread and made a dress for my baby on my own. Americans made everything so complicated!

Still, Phuong Lien's childhood in America was already so much better than the one I had in Vietnam, and Kathy was a big reason why. I had only sticks and stones for toys, there was never enough to eat, and I had to work so hard from the time I was a child. Phuong Lien had a mobile in her bed to look up at, plenty of food, and the chance to go to a good school.

Kathy always took us to different parks and stores all over Miami. We had seen so much already! She took good care of Phuong Lien, too. She put her on her shoulder when she cried and cried, bouncing her until she was quiet. When Phuong Lien could sit up, Kathy tied a rope to a box and pulled her around the house until both of them fell over with laughter.

I still did not understand Kathy. I did not have the English words to tell her I was thankful. Or that I was frustrated. Or that I was scared. Or that I missed being able to talk to people on my own, without Kathy having to interpret. I was also grateful— grateful for the home Kathy had given me, and for the smiles she and my baby shared.

+ + +

To pay for diapers and clothes for the baby, I started cooking for some of the local Vietnamese, all of whom were refugees like me. I had sold bún bò huế back home; I figured I could do the same here, and Kathy offered to help me. First I needed to save money to buy a big heavy stockpot, which wasn't cheap. Each morning when it was still dark, we would strap Phuong Lien in the backseat of Kathy's car and deliver newspapers. After a few months, we had enough for the pot and some extra bowls.

I cooked the soup, then we drove it 5 miles [8 km] to the home of Luc and Tay, the "cousins" of the big family, who were my first customers. Word spread fast, and soon I had so many customers that I bought a bigger pot and more bowls. I also raised the price of the soup from $3.50 to $5. I was able to help Kathy pay for many of our living expenses and still buy the ingredients for the next batch of soup.

One day as we were driving, we hit a bump in the road. The big pot of bún bò soup base fell over, and the dark liquid immediately flooded the floor. My heart stopped. My last few dollars had gone into making that batch. Now I couldn't earn any money on my own to make a new one. Through tears, I told Kathy, "We need a room."

A "room" was what I had called our stand in the Saigon market, but soon Kathy was saying the word *restaurant*. It had to be a place where I could cook the soup *and* sell it, like in Saigon. I pictured the stand that Sinh and I had set up, with its little table and chairs, and thought that Kathy and I should do the same here.

KATHY:

I *loved* the idea of Tung having her own restaurant to sell soup. Her food was like nothing I had ever tasted, and this would be a perfect way to showcase her talents. We'd never heard of any other Vietnamese eateries in Miami, despite the recent arrival of refugees. Miami's Vietnamese population was almost nonexistent before the war. It seemed like the right time.

I knew it would be my job to handle the logistics: find the space, buy some tables and chairs, maybe take a trip to city hall to tie up a few loose ends. Sure, I said during my last restaurant job that I would never again work in the food industry. That was because I didn't like how that particular establishment was run. Now I felt it was the perfect situation for Tung and me, since we would be in charge.

In the end, none of it went the way I expected. Then again, nothing had gone the way I had expected since Tung moved in with me. I was learning to not have expectations.

I certainly didn't expect the waves of intense love I felt for Phuong Lien. I had never thought this kind of love was in the cards for me. I never wanted to have a family. I was happy making decisions around me, just me, thinking only of myself as I went to a party here, a country there.

I had no idea how much joy I would get out of being *needed*—especially by the baby. I became happier because I had someone to love. I did not expect that having a family would give me purpose and stability, nor did I expect to find a lifelong friend in someone from halfway around the world who could barely speak my language. I did not love Tung in a romantic way, and she certainly didn't love me that way, either. Yet we just fit together perfectly.

Since I was young, I had always imagined that having a family as a woman meant constant cleaning and cooking; it certainly had meant that for my mother and my friends' mothers. I figured it would mean I had no time to do anything I actually liked to do. But in this family, I didn't have to do anything that I wasn't good at: Tung cleaned and cooked and raised Phuong Lien. She was great at all of it, especially once I let her do things her way and focused on what I did best: playing and having fun.

We didn't have a lot of money for toys, but we did have cardboard boxes. As soon as Phuongy was able to sit up by herself, I plopped her into a box, threaded a rope through a hole in the box, and pulled her around the house, like I was pulling a sled on snow. Both of us could do this all day. She laughed and laughed, and so did I. When we tired of that, I got on my knees and put her on my back. "I'm a horse!" I'd yell, galloping all over the place.

Most of all, I loved taking Phuongy and Tung to the playground, an experience that was as new to Tung as it was to Phuongy. The first time, both of them looked at the swing set with wide eyes. I set Phuongy in a baby swing and gently pushed her back and forth. I told Tung to sit on the regular swing. I gave Tung a big push and watched as her skinny legs flew into the sky. I listened to both Tung and Phuongy laugh, and I laughed, too.

Phuongy was born when I was in grad school. Tung quit her job to take care of the baby. To pay the bills, I drove taxicabs all over Miami, often driving through the night. Eventually I started teaching math at a local high school. We had enough money to support ourselves, and I didn't waste any time worrying about our finances. I always figured that we would make more at some point and everything would work out fine.

In late 1976, my father summoned Tung, Phuong Lien, and me to Virginia. He had been diagnosed with pancreatic cancer and wanted to see us one last time. He admired Tung and her work ethic and was happy that we had become a family. We piled into the car and drove 1,000 miles [1,600 km] north, stopping at restaurants along the way that served rice. After he died about a year later, my mother moved in with us. She found a job as an executive assistant and contributed toward the household expenses. She already considered herself Phuong Lien's grandmother, and I could tell the baby's infectious smile helped her recover from my father's death. When a relative told my mother that Phuongy was not part of our family, my mother quickly shot back: "She is as much mine as any of my grandchildren."

We celebrated Christmas that year as a family of four. Tung knew a little bit about Santa Claus. She called him Ông già Noel (Christmas old man) in Vietnam. We loved looking at the colorful lights at the Dadeland Mall. As we stood in line so that the baby could sit on Santa's lap, Tung peered at the seated figure. He was a very convincing Santa—chubby, twinkle-eyed, a real white beard. I knew she was wondering if he was real. When he moved his hand, Tung jumped!

I talked to Phuongy, who was now almost two, about Santa, telling her that he would visit on his sleigh, come down the chimney, and leave her presents. Tung listened as I spoke, and I could tell she was taking everything I said as fact. She assumed that here in America, a man in a red jacket brought gifts on Christmas.

After we had made my family's traditional oyster stew and attended a Christmas Eve service at church, Tung and Phuong Lien went to sleep. I took my stash of Christmas gifts out of the closet—a blowup playhouse for Phuongy, an apron and utensils for Tung, and a Lladró statue of a little girl for my mother. I laid them out, then filled stockings with nuts, candy canes, and chocolates, and hung them from the fireplace before going to bed.

The next morning, I pretended to be as surprised as Tung was.

+ + +

After the spilled soup incident, I began to daydream big, as I always had. I dreamed of Tung serving her delicious bún bò to a huge dining room of admirers. I dreamed of Americans learning more about the flavors of Vietnam. Of customers leaving work and coming to our restaurant to relax, have good food, drink excellent beer and wine, and talk. Of the restaurant being a place to rest and recharge so people could go back out and fight the world. Of fame, of Tung becoming known for her cooking.

Tung didn't dream of any of that. She just wanted a place to cook and sell soup. She wanted to make money so that she could buy clothes and food. That dream was practical and seemed realistic to her.

Tung learned how to read the words *For Rent*. We saw a lot of potential restaurant spaces that I liked but were too expensive. Then, in early 1978, we stumbled upon a 46 by 13 foot [14 by 4 m] storefront that had been a clothing shop. The walls were covered with holes from hanging racks. The ceiling was falling down. There was no kitchen. But! It was only $350 a month, and it sat across SW Eighth Street from Versailles, a popular Cuban restaurant.

The area was filled with both Cuban and Vietnamese refugees. What's more, we could do a lot of the construction work ourselves. Charlie Riggenbach, a friend who was a retired builder, had promised to help. Standing on the cracked Spanish tile floor, I looked at Tung. She was nodding. "I like this," she said. "Better than in Saigon. Bigger."

We decided to take it. Tung said all she needed was a stove and a pot. I figured that it would be nice to have a floor that was in one piece, too. We figured we'd be up and running in a few months.

Oh, we had no idea. Who knew that in order to build a kitchen, you had to have a fire system, a complex gas line, and a grease trap? Who knew you had to put in a hood—and that our contractor would disappear halfway through the installation process? Who knew that the air conditioning advertised was only one small unit in the back? Who knew that I would have to spend hours trying to figure out which permit we needed for what system? Who knew that we would have to stretch my teaching salary to cover not only living expenses but also rent for the two and a half years it took us to get the restaurant in working order?

Thank goodness for Charlie, who was spending his retirement helping us out. He wanted us to succeed so much that he refused payment and actually funded a lot of the construction supplies out of his own pocket. He also helped me buy maple lumber from a wholesaler and take it to a mill to be cut into planks for the walls.

After I finished teaching each day, Tung and I would go to work on our restaurant. I sawed the wood planks, poured concrete, and put up tile. Charlie and I installed drywall, which Tung sanded and painted. I rounded up two former helicopter mechanics, who had served in Vietnam, and they helped us install our lighting. We found discounted butcher block that we turned into four dining tables, making the legs out of more maple wood.

Then a city inspector arrived. "You need different drywall," he said. "It must be thicker and fire-rated. Call me when you fix it."

We had no choice but to remove the drywall. Guess who had to sand and paint the new drywall again? I sensed that Tung was getting frustrated. I was, too. I couldn't wait to introduce Tung's food to Miami! So when we had the opportunity to cook at the Orange Bowl Parade in January 1980, I jumped at the chance to publicize our dream. I thought nothing of paying the $250 for space in a tent.

We decided to make spring rolls. We were planning to sell more than just soup at the restaurant, so this was a good chance for a test run of another classic Vietnamese dish. Tung did all the cooking herself, at home. She soaked package after package of bean thread noodles and dried mushrooms. She chopped them and gently mixed them with several pounds of ground pork. Patiently and methodically, she soaked one circular rice paper sheet at a time, rolling it around a few tablespoons of the pork filling. She filled tray after tray for our big debut, making about two hundred spring rolls.

We packed them up, along with a big container of nước chấm dipping sauce made of fish sauce and lime juice, a jug of vegetable oil, and a portable gas burner so that Tung could fry the spring rolls in our tent. We put up a sign: "Two Spring Rolls for $3.50."

Football fans lined up at the other vendors all around us for hot dogs and hamburgers. No one wanted to try our food. All we got were a few quizzical looks, with people glancing blankly at our sign. No one knew what spring rolls were.

I tried dropping the price. I tried dropping it some more. Maybe they needed a more familiar name? I started yelling, "Vietnamese hot dogs!" More confused looks. As the parade came to a close and the crowds began to thin, I made a quick decision and started yelling, "Free!"

Sure enough, people started lining up for the spring rolls. I had a great time handing them out and telling them to come see us on Eighth Street. When all the food was gone, I happily whirled around only to see Tung's eyes narrow at me.

"No one paying!" she said.

"It's okay," I answered. What mattered was that we got our name out! So we didn't make money today; we would make money eventually. I considered it a success that so many people now knew who we were—and how delicious Tung's food was. But Tung just saw all of that chopping and rolling and frying, and all the money spent at the grocery store, and the $250 we had paid to be in the tent. "No money. No money," she kept saying, sending daggers in my direction.

+ + +

As we finished construction in the summer of 1980 with our bank account balance lower than ever, we received help just in time: a $12,000 loan from the Small Business Administration. But two more big problems loomed. The first was that we still had no air conditioning in the dining room. Even a small ceiling unit was really expensive to install.

"Just open," Tung said.

"Just open," Charlie said.

I disagreed. The summer Miami heat and humidity was almost worse inside the restaurant than outside. "People are not going to want to sit here in this," I said, adding, "I'll do it myself." I went to the library, got a book on HVAC fundamentals, and put in the air conditioner. As a safeguard, I asked a contractor friend to sign off on my work before the system was inspected.

The second problem was one no one could fix. By the time we were ready to open in August, we rarely saw any Vietnamese refugees. They had all started to move to other neighborhoods and towns. I didn't know who was going to come to our restaurant, but I knew we weren't quitters.

I had just been going with the flow ever since Tung moved in, reacting to what was happening, doing what I thought was right. Now I was drawing a line in the sand. I couldn't properly run the restaurant and teach at the same time, so I decided to leave my day job. When I went to return my key to the school office, Phuongy, who was now four, tagged along. Fear ran through me as we walked down the hallway. I was giving up my health insurance.

I was partly responsible for this little girl, and here I was leaving a secure job with regular hours and vacation time.

I looked down at Phuongy. She reached up and took my hand. *I'm with you, kid*, I thought. *I don't know where we're going, but we're going.* I loved this child, and I was committed to making our unusual family and the restaurant work.

On August 15, 1980, I posted a big sign on our front window that read "Thank You, Lord—We Are Finally Open." Above it was the name Tung had picked out for the restaurant: Hy Vong, Vietnamese for "hope."

Spring Rolls (Chả Giò) with Nước Chấm

Frying the spring rolls twice results in the crispiest wrapper and also allows you to make the rolls in advance and fry them in batches, as Tung did at Hy Vong. For the bean thread noodles, she recommends Pagoda Lungkow Vermicelli.

MAKES ABOUT 26 SPRING ROLLS

1 lb [455 g] ground pork

1¾ oz [50 g] dried bean thread noodles (see headnote), soaked in hot tap water for 7 minutes, drained, and chopped into 1 in [2.5 cm] lengths

1½ oz [45 g] dried wood ear mushrooms (also known as Chinese black fungus; about 1¼ cups), soaked in water for 12 to 24 hours at room temperature, drained, and finely chopped in a food processor

½ small sweet onion, finely chopped

1 Tbsp fish sauce

1 tsp kosher salt

½ tsp black pepper

½ tsp Accent Flavor Enhancer (optional)

26 dried circular spring roll wrappers, 8½ in [21.5 cm] in diameter

Vegetable oil, for frying

Leaves from about 2 heads red leaf lettuce

About 15 mint sprigs

2 tomatoes, thinly sliced

1 cucumber, thinly sliced

About 3 cups [720 ml] Nước Chấm (page 105), for serving

In a large bowl, combine the pork, noodles, mushrooms, onion, fish sauce, salt, pepper, and Accent (if using). Mix the filling thoroughly with your hands.

continued

Fill a large bowl with cold water. Submerge a rice paper wrapper in the water according to the package directions, then immediately lay out on a flat work surface. Spread 2 Tbsp of filling in a 3 in [7.5 cm] horizontal strip along the center of the bottom third of the wrapper. Tuck the right and left sides of wrapper over the meat, then roll up from the bottom. The wrapper should gently hug the meat—don't roll too tightly, or the spring roll will burst during frying. Set the spring roll on a large platter lined with plastic wrap or parchment paper. Repeat with the remaining wrappers and filling.

In a large heavy skillet (Tung uses cast-iron), heat ½ in [12 mm] of oil over medium-high heat until almost smoking, about 350°F [180°C]. Line a large platter with paper towels. When the oil is ready, carefully add 6 to 8 spring rolls to the skillet, seam-side down, and cook until light golden brown, 1 to 2 minutes. Flip over the spring rolls and cook for another 1 to 2 minutes. Transfer to the platter to drain. Repeat with the remaining spring rolls. When they are all at room temperature, cover and refrigerate for at least 20 minutes and up to 5 days before frying again.

When you are ready to finish the spring rolls, in a clean skillet, heat ½ in [12 mm] of oil over medium-high heat until almost smoking, about 350°F [180°C]. Line a large platter with paper towels. When the oil is ready, carefully add 6 to 8 spring rolls to the skillet, seam-side down, and cook until deep golden brown, 1 to 1½ minutes. Flip over the spring rolls and cook 1 to 1½ minutes more. Transfer to the platter to drain. Repeat with the remaining spring rolls.

Wrap each roll in a lettuce leaf along with mint, tomato, and cucumber, as desired. Serve with the nước chấm dipping sauce in a bowl.

Nước Chấm

This classic Vietnamese dipping sauce incorporates savory, tart, and sweet flavors. Tung chooses to highlight savory and tart: Her version uses far less sugar than you may find in other recipes. Nước chấm is essential for Tung's Spring Rolls (Chả Giò; page 103), Fish with Mango Sauce (page 126), Barbecued Pork with Rice Noodles (Bún Thịt Nướng; page 182), and Pork Rolling Cakes (Bánh Cuốn; page 199).

MAKES ABOUT 3 CUPS [720 ML]

4 large garlic cloves, chopped

½ cup plus 1 tablespoon [135 ml] fish sauce

2 tablespoons plus ½ teaspoon sugar

¼ cup [60 ml] lime juice

In a medium bowl, stir together the garlic, fish sauce, sugar, and 2 cups [480 ml] of water until the sugar is dissolved. Add the lime juice and stir again. The sauce will keep, in an airtight container, in the refrigerator for up to 4 weeks. Stir before using.

CHAPTER 9

Hope Is Alive

Miami, early 1980s

MIAMI HERALD, SEPTEMBER 11, 1980:

"The restaurant's name is Hy Vong, which means 'hope' in Viet-namese. But it gives us more than hope, because this tiny droplet in the swift current of SW Eighth Street in Little Havana proves that our town is invigorating and alive.

The 14-seat restaurant is the enterprise of two women and a 4-year-old daughter. One, the cook, fled Vietnam only moments before the fall, arriving in the United States in 1975. . . . The American who helped her here is waitress and guide to Viet-namese cooking.

That they should become friends and partners in the melt-ing pot that is South Florida is heady spice to all of our lives.

It is even better to report, however, that the food at Hy Vong is excitingly good."

TUNG:

Kathy read me the words in the newspaper. I did not understand most of them, but I understood what was important. The Americans liked my food!

As soon as the review was printed, we got so many customers. They came through the door and ordered my soups, chicken and ginger, and barbecued pork with vermicelli. Their plates came back clean! That made me so happy. I was too busy cooking to talk to them, but I liked how the restaurant gave me a chance to be around other Americans. I liked when they said hello. I wanted to learn from other people besides Kathy.

I had a job. I had my own kitchen and my own space to serve customers. I had a big alley behind the restaurant where I could fillet fish and grill pork. Best of all, I was still able to see Phuong Lien a lot. She went to preschool during the day, then Kathy would bring her to Hy Vong. She'd help me peel carrots, read books at a table, then crawl onto a shelf under the silverware tray and take a nap until Kathy's mother came to take her home.

Every day, I said thanks. *Thank you, Bà Nội. Thank you, Trời.*

And now: *Thank you*, Miami Herald.

+ + +

There was just so much I didn't understand.

I didn't understand why it had taken so much time and work to open a restaurant in America, when selling soup had been so simple in Vietnam. And now that Hy Vong was open, I didn't understand why we weren't making a profit. We had so many customers. We sold so much food. When I was this busy in Saigon, Sinh and I had big fistfuls of bills at the end of the day. We sent money home to our families. I was able to support my mother and six siblings.

At the end of each night, I asked Kathy, "How much did we make?"

Kathy would reply, "I don't know. I haven't counted the money yet."

I shook my head. "We are busy. People know Vietnamese food now. Raise prices!"

I didn't understand why Kathy needed the man helping her in the dining room. Or why she had to buy beer and wine when we didn't have the right permit to sell alcohol and had to give it away for free! That made me so mad. She just waved me off and said, "Don't worry." She always said that when something went wrong. How could I not worry?

I'll never forget the night she showed up right before opening and there was no electricity. Customers were starting to arrive and the dining room was dark and hot, just like the kitchen, where I'd been prepping for service alone for hours, dripping with sweat. Kathy looked at all the people and instructed: "We have to open. Keep cooking."

I had pushed and pushed myself, and my body was just so tired and hot. I took a pan and hit it hard on the kitchen counter. "*You* take over!" I yelled at her. "*You* cook!" That was it. I was done. I stormed out the back door, leaving everyone waiting for their food. "I'm sorry, customers," I said to myself. "I'll see you tomorrow."

I didn't know how to drive. Kathy always drove me everywhere, including home after work, but this time I was not waiting. So I started walking. I walked down busy Douglas Road. I walked down US Highway 1 South. I walked by a gas station and was about to pass a 7-Eleven store when a man suddenly grabbed my purse off my arm. I never heard him come up behind me.

"Help me! Help me!" I screamed. Thankfully, two men immediately ran out of the store, spotted the thief, and yelled at him to drop my purse. I guess he didn't want a chase because he threw it on the ground and ran away. One of the men made sure I was okay, then called the police. I was grateful that, by this point, I could understand and speak basic English. While he waited with me, he asked where I lived.

"South Miami," I said.

"Then why are you walking here? It's so far from home."

"The lady I work with has a big mouth," I replied.

After the policeman took my report, an employee at the 7-Eleven called me a taxi. The fare home cost $5. I gave the driver $7 because people seemed to pay more than the bill in this country. I loved it when Americans did that in our restaurant. But why was everything else so hard? Why didn't Kathy tell me it would be this hard to open a restaurant here? Why didn't she care about making money?

KATHY:

Tung thought the whole point of Hy Vong was to make lots of money. I thought the whole point of the restaurant was to showcase Tung's amazing cooking. To make our customers happy. To give them a place to relax. And to pay our living expenses. All of that, to me, defined success.

One customer told me that she had been undergoing chemotherapy and hadn't had much of an appetite, but when she tasted Tung's food, it was so good she ate more than she had in months! That was why I loved Hy Vong.

Even though I knew that Tung had struggled for financial stability her entire life, it was hard for me to understand just how important money was to her. Because I ran the business end of Hy Vong, Tung held me responsible for the fact that we weren't making much. Yes, our prices were low. They were low because we were the first Vietnamese restaurant in Miami that we knew of, and I didn't think people would pay much for food they weren't familiar with. Remember the Orange Bowl experience?

I also didn't think people would pay much to sit in our humble dining room. Our small menu was initially written on a blackboard, in both English and Vietnamese. Our four bare-topped wooden tables were inches away from each other, and customers sat on folding chairs. To go to our bathroom, they had to walk out the back door and through the alley, sometimes stepping around Tung filleting fish on a cooler. During Miami's frequent thunderstorms, the alley filled with rainwater. On those occasions, women headed to the bathroom often took off their shoes, and our busboy held an umbrella over their heads.

Hy Vong may have been nicer than anywhere Tung had cooked in Vietnam, but it wasn't entirely comfortable by American standards. So when Tung said, "Raise prices! Charge more!" I didn't listen.

We also had no money for advertising. If the *Miami Herald* hadn't written about us so soon and so often, we could have sat for years with only a few customers here and there. The media attention resulted in a constant stream of curious customers, but we could seat only fourteen of them at a time. And because Tung cooked everything by herself and from scratch, we couldn't turn over the tables quickly.

We took in maybe $400 a day, if we were lucky. And that was before our expenses. I bought the best of everything because I didn't think you could make exquisite food with average ingredients. I had to pay a fair wage to our two hardworking employees, a dishwasher and a busboy. After I paid Phuongy's preschool bill, I juggled who should get the rest of the money. The beer and wine distributor? The electric company? The water company? The telephone company?

When our utilities were shut off, despite the inconvenience, there was usually a way around that. We got water at the minimart down the street, and eventually I bought a plumber's key that allowed me to turn the water back on myself. If the water company took the next step and wrapped a wire around the water switch, I cut it with a wire cutter. When the electricity was turned off, I lit candles. Unfortunately, no electricity meant no air conditioning, and I couldn't do anything about that.

Through it all, the same customers kept coming back, again and again. They stuck with us through everything—even Tung deserting the kitchen, which happened more than once in the early days. It wasn't long before they were volunteering to help out however they could. They knew we had a barebones staff, so they picked up ice at the corner store for us, carried anything heavy, and even occasionally bussed their own tables. They shared plates of food with each other when Tung was backed up in the kitchen. When I told them beer and wine was free until we got our liquor license, they gave us generous tips.

"The food was unlike any I had ever tasted," remembers one of our earliest customers, Carl Sugarman. "It was almost a privilege to get a table." After Carl saw Phuong Lien for the first time and realized how much we needed Hy Vong to succeed, he says he got "on the bandwagon to help that child."

As it turns out, our customers didn't really care about our bare-bones setup. As Samuel Blum, another early customer, put it, the restaurant was "so small and it had no atmosphere, but it was incredibly authentic. It was exciting and it was different and it was fun."

We *were* having fun in our laid-back dining room—much more fun than in any restaurant I had ever been in or worked at. I was in charge and I made sure of it! We welcomed everyone, no matter who they were or how little they knew about Vietnamese food. There was no reason to feel intimidated here.

I spent the whole night talking to customers; getting to know them and their families, their likes and dislikes; and helping them navigate the short menu. I explained the flavor of lemongrass, and how we grew the long stalks in our garden at home because we couldn't find it in stores. I explained why Tung used fish sauce, and how it didn't necessarily make dishes taste fishy. I explained what type of bones Tung threw into her huge stockpot, and how using so many bones created such a flavorful broth.

I also challenged people to try new things: I told them I would give them the dish for free if they didn't like it. Every time

Tung overheard me saying this, she would reprimand me. "Don't worry!" I told her. I knew I was creating customers for life.

As it turned out, we never catered to Vietnamese refugees, who turned out to be tough customers. They did come, but after they walked in and saw me, most of them hesitated for a few moments and then headed back out. I assumed they were suspicious of any Vietnamese restaurant with a white woman in the dining room. My busboy and I used to bet on whether they would stay or go.

Little Phuong Lien became one of our biggest assets. She could charm even the gruffest of customers and helped lighten the mood when things were particularly chaotic. Once, when she was about five years old, she walked up to a regular and said earnestly: "The service is going to be very slow tonight. My mother is in a bad mood."

+ + +

Tung had gotten her green card a few years after arriving in Miami, then became a U.S. citizen in 1983. She failed the citizenship test the first time she took it, so Phuong Lien and I helped her study more for the next one. We taught her the word *Congress* by having her memorize *con* (the Vietnamese word for child) and *dress*, which was something that she'd sewn for Phuong Lien. To learn then-President Ronald Reagan's name, we used the word *dragon* because with her accent, it sounded like *Reagan*. Phuong Lien tried to accompany her mother to the second interview, but the agent waved her finger no. Tung managed to pass on her own.

The next step was to get her driver's license. On Tung's first try parallel parking, she smacked into the cone behind her. On her second try, she hit the cone in front. Both times she arrived home from the Department of Motor Vehicles, Phuongy and I heard the front door slam shut. After the third try, we heard the door slam and whispered to each other, "Not today." After the fourth try, the slam was even louder; we just looked at each other and giggled.

When Tung returned from the fifth try, Phuongy and I braced ourselves. We heard the door open, then shut gently. We looked at each other in excitement and dashed into the living room to greet the new driver!

We had two cars, including my mother's, so Tung getting her license made our lives much easier, since we kept different hours at the restaurant. But she now faced a new challenge: navigating. One day we drove separately to get a swing for Phuong Lien. On trips to new places, Tung usually followed me in her car until she learned the route. During this trip, she wanted to go home before we were finished shopping, so I pointed her to the highway and told her to "go straight" until she recognized our exit. When Phuong Lien and I got home a little later, Tung was not there. We figured she had made a stop somewhere.

A few hours later, we heard her come in and slam the door. It turned out she had gone straight for so long that she had ended up in North Miami Beach, about 15 miles [24 km] away. Then she pulled over in confusion and called a tow truck to tow her home. Phuong Lien and I couldn't help but laugh. Eventually Tung did, too.

Fortunately she no longer needed help navigating the aisles during her frequent trips to various grocery stores. She was also getting more comfortable experimenting with unfamiliar ingredients that piqued her curiosity. It didn't matter if it came in commercial packaging and she didn't know exactly what it was or what the instructions said because she still couldn't read many English words.

This is how I once came home to find that Tung had purchased Hidden Valley Ranch salad dressing mix. Having thrown away the directions, which were of no use to her, she smelled the powder, then instinctively added water, sugar, salt, and oil. Once combined, the watery substance bore no resemblance to the ranch dressing I knew. "I think you're supposed to add mayonnaise," I told her. She ignored me.

The next thing I knew, she was stirring up that same watery substance at the restaurant. To my surprise, it tasted great when she tossed it with watercress, sliced avocado, and tomatoes. And when customers tasted it, they couldn't get enough. They started coming back just for that salad. They begged us to sell them jars of the dressing, and we happily obliged. When we shared the fact that it was low-calorie, we couldn't mix it up fast enough.

Although many tried, no customer ever correctly guessed all of the ingredients. Many people assumed it might contain fish sauce, but the truth is there was nothing Vietnamese about the dressing, or the salad. It was 100 percent Tung embracing America.

Watercress Salad with Hy Vong's Signature Dressing

This leafy salad is particularly good with generous amounts of dressing. When peeling the cucumber, use a serrated peeler if you have one for a prettier effect.

MAKES 4 LARGE OR 8 SIDE SALADS

1 bunch watercress, stemmed and chopped

½ head iceberg lettuce, halved lengthwise, cored, and sliced crosswise into 2 in [5 cm] pieces

1 heaping cup [40 to 45 g] roughly chopped cilantro, mint, and/or basil, leaves and stems

1 cucumber, preferably English, peeled and cut into ½ in [12 mm] thick diagonal slices

1 regular avocado, or ½ large Florida avocado, cut into 1 in [2.5 cm] thick wedges

1 large tomato, halved lengthwise and sliced

2 to 3 cups [480 to 720 ml] Hy Vong's Signature Salad Dressing (page 132)

In a large bowl, toss together the watercress, lettuce, and cilantro. Divide among bowls, followed by the cucumber, avocado, and tomato. Serve with at least ½ cup [120 ml] of dressing for each larger salad and ¼ cup [60 ml] of dressing for smaller salads.

Hy Vong's Signature Dressing

Our customers have long speculated about the ingredients in our house salad dressing. This is the first time the full recipe has been published. Its high water content and unusual use of dried Hidden Valley Ranch mix may come as a surprise. Many customers loved it on much more than salad, using it as a dip for spring rolls and raw vegetables.

MAKES ABOUT 4¾ CUPS [1.1 L]

1 oz [28 g] packet Hidden Valley Original Ranch Seasoning, Salad Dressing & Recipe Mix

¼ cup plus 2 Tbsp [90 ml] white vinegar

¼ cup [50 g] sugar

2 Tbsp kosher salt

3 Tbsp vegetable oil

In a large bowl, whisk together the salad dressing mix and 4 cups [960 ml] of water until the mix is dissolved. Whisk in the vinegar, sugar, salt, and, gradually, the oil. The dressing will keep, in an airtight container, in the refrigerator for up to 1 month. Whisk before using.

CHAPTER 10

Partners

Miami, 1980s

TUNG:

I started to write letters to my mother as soon as I got to Kathy's house. I kept picking up pieces of paper and starting to write, then crying so hard that I had to stop. Each time I wrote a word, I would see the image of my mother trying to sell one of my brothers. Or I would think of her tight, worried face. Finally, I managed to scrawl out in Vietnamese that I was in America. "I'm sorry. I went away. I'm okay. I hope I see you one day."

Kathy helped me mail it, but after a few months, it ended up back in our mailbox, marked "Returned." I threw out that letter and started again. When the second letter came back, I threw it out and wrote another. And another, about every two weeks for years. "I am sorry. I am okay. Are you okay? America is wonderful. I am doing wonderful." The United States did not have diplomatic relations with Vietnam at the time, so apparently a lot of mail wasn't getting through. I also wasn't sure if my family was still at the same address. I could only hope that, eventually, one of my letters would make it.

After Phuong Lien was born, I sent a letter telling my mother I now had a daughter. I knew I had brought shame on her for leaving, and that there would be more shame when she learned I had had sex with a man without marrying him. Still, I wanted to share the news with her.

As expected, that letter came back, too, as did one in which I told her we had opened Hy Vong. Kathy saw my sadness and suggested trying something new. She said she would send one of my letters to her friend in Austria, who would then mail it to my mother from her local post office. Before we sealed my envelope, Kathy inserted a Hy Vong business card.

+ + +

I never told my mother anything about Minh. But as Phuong Lien got older, I started to think that maybe I should tell *her* about her father. What would I say? It was too much to tell a little girl how both of us had no one at the camp; how I felt so empty; how I accepted the ring he offered me, but could not put it on my finger; how hurt I felt when he gave another woman a coat instead of me.

After Phuong Lien turned six, I decided to try. I looked into her eyes and began to speak, but as soon as I thought back to that man, my stomach clenched, my throat turned dry, and I started to cry. I couldn't stop. The pain was too great. Phuong Lien's eyes got wide and tears started to run down her face, too. We cried together, and I could say nothing more.

That fear in my daughter's eyes when she saw me cry haunted me and made me decide not to tell her the truth. She shouldn't grow up with that kind of shame and knowledge, or any worry that that terrible man would someday come and find us.

Instead, not long after, I told her another story—the same story I told to customers, newspaper reporters, and anyone else who asked. *Phuong Lien, you have a father. He was a soldier in the*

South Vietnamese Army and he died in the war in Vietnam. I was pregnant with you when I escaped in a boat and now I am here. You are an American.

+ + +

Late one night in March 1985, my hands were deep in soapy water after dinner service at Hy Vong when I heard someone come in the front door and ask Kathy for me. I wiped my hands and walked out of the kitchen to find a young Vietnamese woman. She said her name was Tran and asked in Vietnamese, "Where are you from?"

"Điện Bàn. Quảng Nam," I answered, telling her the name of my village and province.

She nodded, then said, "Your mother got your letter."

I began to shake. My knees buckled and I grabbed the nearest table for support. Was this real?

Tran said she was also from the Điện Bàn area and now lived in Miami. When she went home recently to visit relatives, my mother heard that someone was visiting from America. She found Tran and showed her the business card that Kathy had put in the letter we mailed to Austria several months earlier. "You are from America?" my mother asked Tran. "Do you know my daughter?"

Tran told me that about six months after the war ended, my mother sent my brother to Saigon to look for me. When he couldn't find me, they assumed that I was dead and began to mourn. They moved the only picture of me that they had—taken when I was about five—and hung it in our brick house above the tiny shelf that served as the family altar. They burned incense in my memory and, despite their constant hunger, kept a few precious grains of rice on the shelf as an offering for my spirit.

Ten years passed with my family thinking I was dead. Then, one day, my mother received my letter that Kathy's friend had mailed. When my brother read her the letter, which said I was in "America," she thought that must be a small village in another country. Even after she read my note, she wasn't sure whether to believe that it was really from me, that I was actually alive.

Tran recognized the name of our restaurant on the card right away. She had read about Hy Vong in the newspaper. She told my mother that not only was I alive, I was in charge of a well-known restaurant. My mother replied: "Tell my daughter to come visit our family one day." She also had one of my brothers write a letter to me, and asked Tran to bring it to me at Hy Vong.

Tran handed me a piece of paper. Through tears, I recognized my brother's handwriting.

Everyone was well. My family was still together. No one had been sold. He also wrote that our land had been turned into a hợp tác xã, a communist-run cooperative farm. As such, my mother's house now had a more precise address, which he shared with me in the hope that my future letters would have a better chance of reaching them.

I cried so hard I could hardly see. I threw my arms around Tran, barely able to choke out the words, "Thank you."

Immediately, I wrote another letter to my mother. "I'm okay. I have a daughter, Phuong Lien. I live with Kathy, an American lady, and Kathy's mother. How are you? Everyone take care. Don't worry about me."

KATHY:

It had to have been more than coincidence. Tran could have lived anywhere in America, but she happened to live right here in our city. She could have had family anywhere in Vietnam, but her family happened to live right in Tung's tiny village. "Trời có mắt," Tung and I said to each other, over and over. "God has eyes."

The letter brought Tung much relief. She had been so desperate for her mother to know she was fine, and to share the news that she now had a daughter of her own. After that happened, she carried herself more lightly, smiled more often. Seeing that, I couldn't help but think about the complicated bond between a mother and daughter, and my own relationship with Phuongy.

Even though having Phuongy in my life was the closest I would ever come to having a daughter, I never, ever tried to be her mother. I didn't want to be a mother, and Phuongy already had a mother, a great mother. I was always grateful to Tung for sharing Phuongy—there was nothing I would rather do than spend time with her. I made sure that Tung got all of the praise for everything Phuongy accomplished and had all of the authority over what she was permitted to do and know.

When Phuongy was six, she told me, "I don't have a father." I tried to laugh it off. "Everyone has a father," I told her. "I hear he's ugly. You look like him," I teased, which made her laugh. When Tung told Phuong Lien that her father had died in the war, I just went along with it. It was her decision to make, not mine.

Phuongy always got my jokes. And it was obvious as soon as she was able to talk that she was a lot wiser than I was. Whether I complained to her about a store not having the produce I needed, or confided in her that Tung was mad at me, Phuongy almost always had a solution. She was like her mother that way.

In fact, mother and daughter reminded me of each other a lot. From the age of five, Phuongy took dance lessons at the Martha Mahr School of Ballet, which was conveniently located next door to our butcher shop. She became quite good, eventually graduating to pointe shoes.

Whenever I saw Phuong Lien's graceful dancing, I pictured Tung's movements in the kitchen. I could watch both of them all day. Phuong Lien's long arms and fingers made such beautiful lines through the air. She carefully controlled each elegant move. Tung, too, moved with elegance in the kitchen. Her chopping was precise, her stirring was smooth. It was a quiet harmony between the ingredients and her cooking. I watched other chefs on TV and they were full of jerky, sudden movements. Tung's movements were all poise and rhythm.

+++

As Tung became more confident in the kitchen, she began experimenting with more flavors and textures. I loved learning about food and had been collecting cookbooks and reading food magazines for a long time, so having a roommate and business partner like Tung was really exciting. It also inspired me to cook more.

After learning that Vietnamese eat fried or steamed fish with a side of unripe green mango and fish sauce, all garnished with herbs, I happened to see a recipe for fish with mango and green peppercorns in a magazine, and decided to make it with beautiful ripe local fruit.

I thought the dish turned out delicious, until I presented it to Tung, who shot me the same disdainful look she had given me all those years ago when she was unsatisfied with her phở. She then set about trying her own take on the dish. She bought more snapper and ripe mango and got to work.

I watched as she basically followed the same steps I had, then her instinct kicked in and she added fish sauce and a little butter at the very end. What a difference that made! Those two simple additions amplified how the soft, sweet mango complemented the tart, spicy peppercorns, picked while they were still green and young. Mango and peppercorns—so different, yet somehow so right together.

I started tearing out magazine recipes and leaving them in places where I knew Tung would see them. I became particularly drawn to a recipe for chicken breasts wrapped in puff pastry with butter and cream cheese, and headed to the kitchen again. Tung came in after I pulled the tray out of the oven, saw the unwieldy packages with white filling oozing out, and shook her head. "Too big," she said. We both knew she could do better.

She cut the chicken into smaller pieces and marinated it in fish sauce. Next, she blended garlic and watercress into the cream cheese and tucked it inside the pastry with the chicken. Right before she served it, she spread more of the cream cheese mixture across the top of the hot baked pastry, turning it into a sauce. Now the chicken was more tender and flavorful, and the sharp watercress softened the richness of the pastry, which was folded much more neatly than mine.

Both the fish with mango and chicken in pastry ended up on Hy Vong's menu—and helped put us on the map. We were fortunate and relieved that our business kept growing, mostly by word of mouth. A few months after we opened, we had long, long lines of people outside our front door pretty much every night except Monday, when we were closed. In order to keep things as orderly as possible, I had to put out a notepad for people to write their names on, along with how many were in their party.

Everyone was treated the same, including the many celebrities and famous people who visited. I didn't care who our guests were. I wanted Hy Vong to be a place where people could just be. I wanted them to know that at Hy Vong, we celebrated whom they were as people—not their status, color, sexual orientation, or anything else about them.

Maybe that was part of the restaurant's appeal. More than once, a gay couple on a date told me we were much more welcoming than other restaurants. When many of them winked at me and asked, "How's your partner, Kathy?" I always told them that Tung was fine, thank you. I did consider Tung my partner, in business and in life. I considered her my family, even though we didn't love each other romantically. As for a sexual partner, by then I had decided that celibacy worked best for me: All of my customers' romances reminded me of soap operas. And besides, I was married to Hy Vong.

Only Phuong Lien understood. Ever the insightful one, she was just eleven years old when she told me flatly, "I don't see you getting married."

+ + +

While I had all the family I needed in Tung, Phuongy, and our customers, Tung was still reconciling her ideas of a traditional Vietnamese family. One of the few Vietnamese customers we had at Hy Vong was an older woman named Hang. Hang and Tung became close friends. Tung didn't know many other Vietnamese people, so Hang represented one of the few remaining ties to her culture.

I knew that Hang had been pressuring Tung to get married, as one would expect from a Vietnamese of her generation. When Hang suggested that Tung meet a single man who lived in the same apartment building as her children in Orlando, I didn't say anything. I figured I was there if she needed me, but I wasn't going to tell her how to live. However, I did take the drive with her up I-95 North to meet Bao.

From Tung's perspective, it was a good match. Bao was from a rural area near Điện Bàn and had been a farmer, like Tung. From my perspective, it was a disaster in the making. Bao seemed unstable, and I just kept thinking of what had happened in the refugee camp, with Tung following the Hoangs' advice to get together with Minh. Now it was Hang pushing Bao on Tung, and I feared that Tung wasn't viewing the situation with nearly enough skepticism.

I didn't try to dissuade her, though, because that could have wrecked our relationship. Tung wanted to make her own decisions. She wanted more independence from me. She wasn't content with the family we had built at home and at the restaurant. She wanted a marriage that would give her her own Vietnamese family. She once told me that her culture considered women old maids if they didn't get married by the age of thirty. She was thirty-eight when she met Bao.

In a matter of months, Tung and Bao were married in a ceremony at the Lutheran church we occasionally attended in the Coral Gables neighborhood of Miami. One of my sisters sewed Tung a traditional big, white American-style wedding dress for the ceremony, and Tung bought a Vietnamese wedding dress for the reception, which was held at the Coral Gables Woman's Club, across the street from the church. She cooked all of the food herself in advance for the more than one hundred guests, which included many Hy Vong customers. I felt that a lot of the guests were looking curiously at me, wondering how I fit in this picture.

Bao paid for the wedding and the honeymoon in Hawaii. When they left, Phuongy and I stood on the lawn to wave goodbye. Phuongy had been silent most of the day, but as the car drove off, she said, "You said you'd never leave me."

I looked at her. I took her hand. "I meant it," I said. "I will never leave you."

Fish with Mango Sauce

We particularly like this mango sauce with fried snapper or grouper, but you can serve it over any kind of fish prepared any way you'd like, such as steamed, baked, or broiled. Feel free to add more peppercorns, mango, or nước chấm to suit your taste. Green peppercorns in brine can be found at some grocery stores and online.

SERVES 4

3 Tbsp unsalted butter

1½ ripe mangoes, peeled and very thinly sliced

1½ tsp green peppercorns in brine, drained

1½ tsp fish sauce

3 Tbsp heavy cream

Vegetable oil, for frying

2 lb [910 g] white fish fillets,
such as snapper or grouper, skin removed

¾ cup [180 ml] Nước Chấm (page 105),
gently warmed if it has been refrigerated

2 green onions, thinly sliced, for garnish

In a small pot, melt the butter over low heat. (You can also do this in a small bowl in the microwave.) Add the mango, peppercorns, and fish sauce, gently mix together, and let cool. Add the heavy cream, gently mix, and set aside.

In a large heavy skillet, heat 1 in [2.5 cm] of oil over medium-high heat until almost smoking, about 350°F [180°C]. Carefully add the fillets to the pan, then immediately push a spatula under each fillet so the fish does not stick to the bottom of the pan. Cook, flipping once, until cooked through, 2 to 4 minutes per side, depending on the fillets' size. Transfer the fillets to plates or one large platter, draining any excess oil first, if needed. Top with the reserved mango sauce, the nước chấm, and green onions.

Chicken in Pastry

Feel free to make these ahead, as we did at Hy Vong. You can refrigerate the fully baked pastries for up to 4 days. To serve, reheat at 300°F [150°C] for about 30 minutes, then top with the remaining sauce and green onions.

SERVES 4

1 small sweet onion, finely chopped

¼ cup [60 ml] fish sauce

1 Tbsp lime juice

1 tsp sugar

½ tsp black pepper

2 boneless, skinless chicken breasts, about 1¼ lb [570 g] total, halved crosswise

2 large garlic cloves

4 oz [115 g] watercress (about ½ bunch)

Two 8 oz [230 g] packages cream cheese

⅛ tsp salt

One 1 lb [455 g] box of 2 frozen puff pastry sheets, defrosted

1 large egg, beaten

2 green onions, sliced, for garnish

Preheat the oven to 350°F [180°C], with a rack in the middle position. If available, use the convection setting.

Meanwhile, in a large bowl, combine the sweet onion, fish sauce, lime juice, sugar, and pepper. Cut a small slit about halfway through the flesh of the top of each chicken piece to help the marinade penetrate the meat. Add the chicken to the onion mixture, toss to coat, and let sit for about 30 minutes.

Meanwhile, chop the garlic in the bowl of a food processor. Add the watercress, cream cheese, and salt and process until it becomes a creamy sauce. Divide the sauce into two small bowls and set aside.

continued

127

On a lightly floured surface, roll out the first pastry sheet until it's about 10 by 18 in [25 by 46 cm]. Cut that sheet in half, so that you have two pieces measuring about 10 by 9 in [25 by 23 cm]. Cut a 1 in [2.5 cm] wide strip off the shorter side of both pieces, which should then each measure about 9 by 9 in [23 by 23 cm]. Cut both of those strips so they are 4 in [10 cm] long, discarding the excess.

Place one of the strips in the middle of each of the two larger pastry pieces to reinforce the dough. Take one of the bowls of sauce and spread one-fourth of it over each strip. Shake any excess marinade off two pieces of chicken breast, then place one on top of each strip. Fold the top of each sheet down to the middle of the breast and then fold the bottom of the pastry up over the top portion so they overlap; gently stretch them if they don't. Press gently so they stick together.

Fold the sides of pastry in toward the middle so they overlap; gently stretch them if they don't. Press gently so they stick together. Lay the wrapped chicken breasts seam-side down on a baking sheet. Repeat the entire process with the other sheet of pastry, the rest of the sauce from that bowl, and the remaining chicken.

Brush the tops and sides of the pastry with the egg wash, then bake until the pastry is golden brown and the chicken is cooked through (165°F [74°C] on a meat thermometer), about 40 minutes. Let cool for a few minutes, then spread one-fourth of the remaining bowl of sauce on top of each pastry. Garnish with the green onions and serve.

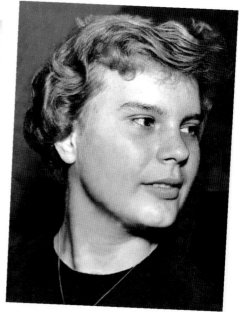

above:
Kathy's Grandma Peterson
(Anna Katherine Peterson),
with two of her great-
grandchildren, early 1960s.

right:
Kathy as a teenager, 1960s.

above:
Tung (left) and her friend, Sinh,
in Saigon, 1974.

right:
The ring Tung's grandmother, whom
she called Bà Nội, passed on to her.

above:
Tung at the Fort Indiantown Gap
refugee camp in Pennsylvania, 1975.

right:
Tung and newborn Phuong Lien,
spring 1976.

above:
Kathy and baby Phuong Lien
playing with a box, 1976.

right:
Tung cooking in the kitchen
at home, 1977.

above:
Phuong Lien with Kathy's mother,
Gwendolyn Manning, whom she
called Grandma, 1979.

right:
Kathy, Phuong Lien, and Tung, 1980.

above:

Celebrating opening after two and a half years of work:
the outside of Hy Vong in the early 1980s.

right:

Hy Vong's business card with
Phuong Lien's picture, 1980s.

above:
Handmade tables
at Hy Vong, early
1980s.

right:
Kathy, Phuong Lien,
and Tung in front of
Hy Vong, taken by
the *Miami Herald*,
1981.

left:
Kathy and Phuong Lien, 1981.

below:
Phuong Lien, Kathy, and Tung cooking at Hy Vong, 1982.

above:
Tung and Phuong Lien
(in a dress sewn by Tung)
on Christmas, 1982.

right:
Kathy and Phuong Lien on
vacation in Yosemite National
Park, 1984.

left:
Phuong Lien in ballet class, 1991.

below:
Tung's mother and brother, Lai, hugging her, Đà Nẵng airport, Vietnam, 1993.

left:
Tung's mother meeting
Phuong Lien for the
first time in Đà Nẵng,
Vietnam, 1993.

below:
Phuong Lien lighting
incense at the grave of
her great-grandfather
(Bà Nội's husband), 1993.

above:
Tung making pork rolling cakes (bánh cuốn)
using a fabric-covered steamer in Vietnam, 1993.

below:
Kathy on the street in Đà Nẵng, Vietnam, 1993.

left:
A dressed-up Tung navigating
a flooded street in Vietnam,
1993.

above:
Phuong Lien and Tung at Phuong
Lien's high school graduation, 1994.

above:
Tung and Kathy sparring
on vacation in William
Shakespeare's birthplace,
Stratford-upon-Avon,
United Kingdom, 1995.

right:
Kathy playing soccer
with children in Điện
Bàn, Vietnam, 1999.

left:
Kathy and Tung in the Hy Vong kitchen, in a photo taken by an appreciative customer, early 2000s.

above:
Lyn (Phuong Lien) and Tung, 2018.
Photo by Libby Volgyes.

CHAPTER 11

Family

Miami, late 1980s to mid-1990s

TUNG:

I lived in America, with Americans. I had earned my American citizenship. I had an American daughter. Each night at the restaurant, I cooked for mostly Americans. American restaurant reviewers wrote that my food was good, some of the best in Miami. I felt good about what I had achieved in America and about myself as an American. But I never forgot where I came from and I missed a lot about my real home.

I didn't talk to Vietnamese people very often. But each time I did, my identity as an American faded into the background. I listened for their accent. If I heard the polished tones of someone who was educated and from a wealthier background, I suddenly became a Vietnamese peasant again. I felt like the child whose parents lived in a hut made of rice-paddy stalks instead of a brick house. I felt like I should be subservient. I felt like I needed to have more in my hand to stand up to them.

That was the case with Bà Hang, a gray-haired refugee from Saigon who would regularly visit me in Hy Vong's kitchen as I got ready for dinner service. She was often the only company I had during those long, lonely hours. As a show of respect, I always added the *Bà* to her first name when I talked to her.

"I have a man for you," Bà Hang said one day, watching as I chopped onions. "He has a good job as a mechanic. He came from Vietnam alone. He has nobody, just like you."

I could see right away what was happening, and I tried to resist. "A lot of refugees lost family," I told her. "A lot of people are alone. I am happy to have Phuong Lien."

"Think about it," Bà Hang insisted. "You don't want to become a *bà cô già*," the Vietnamese term for old maid or spinster.

"I don't think about that," I said. "I am thinking about the restaurant. I have to take care of my daughter."

She persisted, and I began to think it might be okay. As Bà Hang said, in order to be a truly respectable Vietnamese woman, it wasn't enough to just have a child. I needed to have a husband, too. I spent all day and all night at Hy Vong—where else was I going to meet a husband?

Kathy went with me to Orlando to meet Bao. I liked that he, too, was from the countryside. I liked his gentle manner. I enjoyed talking with him in Vietnamese. I felt that he was a better match than Minh would have been. When we decided to get married, I was happy. I decided that Bao, Phuong Lien, and I would continue to live with Kathy and her mother. While Kathy made me frustrated, I knew she was good for my daughter. We just needed more room.

+ + +

The restaurant was always busy, and I had already been saving to move to a newer house, one that I owned. I was tired of living in a house owned by Kathy's mother, who kept everything so messy. I was tired of the piles of newspapers all over the hallway and a

dining room table so cluttered that we could not sit down to eat.
Now that I was married, I wanted to have a bigger, sunnier yard
where I could garden, where I could grow things that reminded me
of Vietnam.

Kathy wanted to move to a neighborhood in the school dis-
trict of Coral Gables High because she said that the high school
would be very good for Phuong Lien, who was eleven at the time.
We found a three-bedroom with a Spanish-tiled roof and a big
backyard that I loved right away. The yard was filled with weeds
and dirt, but I dreamed of filling it with lush tropical plants like
jackfruit and papaya. It was too expensive, though, even with
Kathy's mother's help.

Kathy had been talking to customers about our plans to
move. When one of them, Mike Marks, heard that we could not
afford the house we wanted, he said he would become the sole
lender for our mortgage. It was more money than any bank would
loan us. We were so grateful.

When Mike drew up the papers, he suggested that only
Kathy and I be listed on the mortgage. He thought that Bao should
be left off and potentially added later. Maybe Mike saw the problems with my marriage sooner than I did.

I noticed something was wrong with my new husband
after we all moved to the new house. Bao began talking to him-
self. Often, when I talked to him, he did not respond. He paced
around a lot. If I told him something, he might not remember it the
next day.

"Get a job," I told him over and over. He had quit his job
in Orlando to move to Miami, but there were plenty of mechanic
shops here where he could work. Each night I came home to find
that he hadn't even tried. Before long, he also started to announce,
"I don't love you."

I told Bà Hang, "Bao is worse and worse each day."

"Maybe his behavior was hurt because of what he saw in the
war," she said.

147

Then things started to get scary. Neighbors came up to me as I worked in the yard. "Your husband was peeking into our windows," they told me. One night, he held a kitchen knife raised as if he was going to kill someone. I snuck up behind him and snatched the knife out of his hand. A few days later, I found Bao taking our knives and wandering around the neighborhood; Phuong Lien was the one who saw him and called for help.

He had to leave our house immediately! He was putting us in danger. He went to live with a family he knew from Bà Hang's church. That family decided to send him to a mental hospital. I later found out he had been taking medication for a mental condition before we met, but after he moved in with us, he stopped. That was it, I vowed. I had such terrible luck with relationships. Maybe marriage was just not for me.

"Try again," demanded Bà Hang. "You want to have a family. You won't be accepted by Vietnamese if you don't have a husband. I am watching out for you."

Bà Hang wanted to play matchmaker for me a second time. She thought that if Bao didn't work out, maybe someone else would. She started having a Vietnamese refugee named Duc talk to me.

I really liked Duc. He worked hard. He was a welder during the day and worked at a Chinese restaurant at night. He, too, was alone, having come here with only a friend. After a few months I invited him to move in with us, but I did not want to get married yet. I told him that we could see how things went.

I was an American, but I wanted to belong in the Vietnamese culture. I wanted a family that my mother and brothers and sister in Vietnam would understand and be proud of. Maybe with Duc, I would finally get this family.

KATHY:

At first, I thought Duc would be a much better match for Tung than Bao had ever been. He seemed to treat her better and, like Tung, he was a hard worker. Unfortunately, we soon realized that Duc was spending a lot of his money on gambling. He said he was lonely, had also gambled a lot in Vietnam, and didn't have much of a support system in America. I wondered when Tung would learn to judge people better, when she would learn she was good enough to stand up to Vietnamese people who were from a higher class.

I thought Hang's motives for fixing up Tung were selfish, just as Mrs. Hoang's had been all those years ago in the refugee camp: Hang wanted control over Tung, I thought—maybe even a piece of the restaurant. I wished that Hang could look at Tung and see what I saw: a talented, courageous woman, not a peasant to be taken advantage of.

Tung and Duc eventually broke up, and Duc moved out of our house. Phuongy and I were happy to see him go. Neither of us felt that our family was incomplete.

+ + +

I tried to keep Phuongy's life normal while Tung's relationships imploded. But Phuongy was going through turmoil of her own. Her passion was still ballet. Each day before we served dinner at Hy Vong, I dropped her off at the ballet school for class. When she began dancing on toe shoes around the age of ten, my once-happy girl started to come home from class in tears.

One Monday I stayed to watch her class, since the restaurant was closed. Her teacher pulled me aside and said, "Phuong Lien's arch is not improving. She will probably have flat feet. Find something else for her to do."

Ballet was all Phuong Lien wanted to talk about. Her feet slid into ballet positions everywhere—at home, in line at the grocery store. "Look," I said to her teacher. "I cannot tell her to not dance."

Apparently the teacher could, though. I watched with anger as she kept putting Phuongy in the back of the lineup. No one was going to do this to my little girl! She should be able to have fun without being perfect. She should be allowed to make mistakes. I had certainly made plenty of mistakes all of those years ago when I rode horses and played softball. I fell off a lot of horses. I just tried again.

If Phuong Lien wanted to be a dancer, I was going to help her be a dancer. First, we had to learn how to build a dancer's body. I started reading anatomy books. I drove more than an hour to Florida Atlantic University to find books on alignment. I brought home ugly black-and-white orthopedic shoes that doctors said would help Phuongy's feet. When customers asked, "How is Phuong Lien?" I told them that she was having trouble. Hearing more about the problem, one customer said she had foot issues, too, and handed me the phone number for her Pilates instructor, Dale, on Miami Beach.

I had never heard of Pilates, but we drove out to see Dale anyway. He began helping Phuongy physically and, more importantly, mentally: She started standing taller. She walked into ballet class with more confidence. She worked twice as hard. I'll never forget the moment Phuongy was able to finally do a triple pirouette for the first time. "I did it! I did it!" she screamed, and without asking permission, tore out of the ballet class to hug me in the waiting room.

Eventually, the teacher told me she was wrong about Phuong Lien's feet. They had developed just fine. Phuongy's self-esteem took a while to completely recover, but she remained persistent, and she even danced at a summer camp at the prestigious Joffrey Ballet School in New York.

When it came to Phuong Lien, I realized I really needed to stand up to people. If I didn't, my child might not have the best chance to realize her dreams. Helping Phuong Lien overcome that dance struggle was the beginning of feeling more comfortable in my own skin. When I helped my family become happier, I became happier, too.

+ + +

What also made me happy was seeing the community we were building at Hy Vong. Customers came home from their vacations with souvenirs for us, invited us to their children's school plays and graduations, and shared personal successes and disappointments. Regulars got to know each other, chatting between tables, and offered us more support and advice than we ever could have imagined.

Mike, of course, lent us money, and helped us negotiate a lease renewal. Several customers encouraged me to raise our prices. Mark Riedmiller was one of them. He said he and his wife loved Tung's food so much that they wanted to make sure we made enough money to stay in business. He called us "nice people who were more focused on food than on the business end of the business." Mark also did us a favor when he asked me if I knew what a corkage fee was. I did not.

"That's a fee to open and maintain somebody's wine," Mark said. "For God's sake, charge it."

"What if people can't afford that?" I asked. "What if they stop coming?" We had finally gotten a license to sell our own wine, but people still liked to bring their own.

Mark told me that many of our customers were wealthy—"they have leather totes for wine!"—and that it was a small price to pay for Tung's food. Eventually, he talked me into charging a fifteen-dollar corkage fee per bottle, which definitely helped our bottom line.

When it started to take hours to get a table, one customer brought us a beautiful wooden bench engraved with "Hy Vong" to put outside the front door so people would have a place to sit while they waited. According to another customer, Debra Lundy, the waits for a table were frustrating, but worth it.

"People who went on the same night every week knew each other," she shared. "People would talk to each other. The food was fabulous, when you got it, and you just had to have the frame of mind of what you were getting yourself into. If you got out early, it was a bonus. If someone came in who didn't know any better and said 'I'm going to a movie,' we'd go, 'You're in the wrong restaurant, honey.'"

Debra was happy to wait with the likes of Billy Joel, Gloria Estefan, Lauren Hutton, Jorge Villamizar, and Univision host Raúl De Molina, among others. No one got to jump the line. Most of the time, I didn't even know who the celebrities were. When anyone got mad at me for the wait—or were rude to me or other customers—I had no problem kicking them out.

After I kicked out one particularly rude person, another customer ran up to me and said, "Kathy, do you know what you just did?"

"No," I said.

"You just told the mayor of Miami that Burger King was down the street!"

I shrugged it off. I would treat anyone well, so long as they treated my guests and me well. If they were rude? Well, then they didn't deserve to eat Tung's food.

I started to gain something of a reputation: one *Miami Herald* writer called me "a cross between a disoriented cat lady and the Soup Nazi from *Seinfeld*." My customers told me they were horrified by this description. I just laughed. I certainly had been called worse. In fact, I was often called worse by Tung!

+ + +

In the early '90s, when I heard that many of the Thai restaurants in Miami were serving squid, I thought we should, too. Only better. Who cared if squid wasn't a common restaurant dish at the time? I could convince people that it was worth eating. I had a reputation for that, too. A *Miami Herald* critic had written this a few years earlier: "Manning will invariably be there to take your order, and she is the best guide to Vietnamese cuisine you could ever want to encounter. Let her steer you around the menu."

So what if squid tentacles scared people? We could cut them off. What did it matter that we couldn't even buy cleaned squid? Tung could handle that part. What I didn't want to do was fry it like the Thai restaurants.

"Boil the squid," suggested Tung, who had seen that done in Vietnam.

I shook my head. "Americans aren't going to eat plain boiled squid," I said. That was just too bland. Maybe a tangy sauce would help? I started playing around with lime juice, vinegar, and soy sauce. Meanwhile, Tung experimented with ways to boil the squid so that it would have more flavor, adding things like ginger and fish sauce to the cooking liquid.

After we perfected our dish, I tried to sell it to a couple that came in frequently. "The special tonight is squid salad," I said.

They looked at each other, noses wrinkling. "I don't eat calamari," said the man.

I was ready for this response. "Try it," I said. "It's *so* good. If you don't like it, I won't charge you."

Tung heard me say this and, as usual, shot me a glare. Still, she plated the salad beautifully, heaping the squid rings with fresh herbs and dousing everything in the soy-lime sauce. I set it on the table, then had to duck back into the kitchen to pick up a few more orders. After I delivered those, I circled back to the couple. "How did you like it?" I asked.

"Wow. That is *so good!*" they said in unison. Then they pointed to another table across the room, where I saw their empty plate. The couple had exclaimed so much over the dish that the other diners wanted a taste, too. After the plate made its rounds, everyone was trying to get my attention to order their own squid salads.

"If Kathy says it's good," the customers agreed, "it's good."

Squid Salad

This is one of our easiest dishes to make and it packs enormous flavor.

SERVES 4 AS AN APPETIZER

2½ lb [1.2 kg] squid bodies (not tentacles),
peeled and rinsed

¾ oz [20 g] ginger (about a 1 in [2.5 cm] long piece),
peeled and julienned

1 Tbsp fish sauce

1 tsp kosher salt

½ tsp black pepper

½ cup [120 ml] lime juice

½ cup [120 ml] white vinegar

¼ cup [60 ml] soy sauce

¼ cup [50 g] sugar

1 small sweet onion, halved lengthwise
and thinly sliced crosswise

2 cups [about 80 g] chopped cilantro, mint, and/or basil

4 handfuls red leaf lettuce, for serving (optional)

¼ cup [35 g] crushed, finely chopped,
or ground dry-roasted unsalted peanuts

Cut the squid crosswise into ¼ in [6 mm] thick pieces, cutting the wider pieces in half, if desired. Transfer the squid to a medium saucepan. Add the ginger, fish sauce, salt, pepper, and ¼ cup [60 ml] of water and stir to combine.

Put the saucepan over high heat and cook, stirring occasionally, until the squid turns white and is just cooked through, about 4 minutes. Transfer the mixture to a medium bowl and allow the squid to cool to room temperature.

Meanwhile, in a small bowl, stir together the lime juice, vinegar, soy sauce, and sugar. When the squid is cool, carefully pour off any excess water, keeping the ginger in the bowl. Add the lime juice mixture, onion, herbs, and peanuts and gently toss to combine. Serve on a bed of lettuce, if you like.

CHAPTER 12

The Biggest Shrimp

Miami, 1988 to 1994

LYN (PHUONG LIEN):

Kathy told me a busboy had called in sick again, which meant that I had to go into Hy Vong that night to bus tables. *Great*, I thought. That meant I had to skip going to the movies with my friends. Social nights like those were the only things holding me together in high school.

By the time I was a teenager, I had come to dread my time at Hy Vong. I winced at the fading paint on the walls, the uncomfortable broken chairs with chipped seats, the tiny, crowded dining room that sat on a big street with heavy traffic whizzing outside. I hoped no one I knew from school would see me clearing dirty plates and wiping down tables.

I parked in the back parking lot, which was strewn with broken glass and lined with barred windows. I walked through the narrow alley to Hy Vong. As usual, the back door was open so that a breeze could waft into the hot, claustrophobic kitchen.

I could hear the simmer of stock cooking on one of the stove's back burners, the radio playing country music, and the busboys setting the tables with a paper placemat, napkin, fork, and knife for each setting before the diners arrived. The kitchen smelled of chicken and onions.

My mother, whom I called Mẹ (the Vietnamese word for mother), was sweating from the heat of the stove. Her hair was pulled back into a messy ponytail, and she wore what I called her "uniform"—a sleeveless shirt, capri pants, and a faded and slightly torn apron tied around her waist with a towel tucked into the side.

"Phuong Lien," Mẹ said, "how was your day?"

I gave her the same answer I always did. "Great. Fun."

She smiled at me and continued working. I walked over to Kathy, who was unloading bags of tomatoes and cucumbers onto the counter. I knew she had spent all day going from store to store to get the freshest ingredients: tomatoes that had never been refrigerated, basil that filled the air with a fresh herbal fragrance.

"Hi, Kathy, I'm here," I told her.

"Hi, Phuongy," she said. "Thank you for coming! How was ballet rehearsal this morning? Did you use your new toe shoes?"

"Rehearsal was good," I replied. "The toe shoes are much better! I have to break them in some more."

The restaurant was about to open for dinner. Kathy had purchased beautiful, enormous shrimp for that night's special, curried shrimp and crabmeat. She wanted to serve four shrimp with each order. Mẹ shook her head at this, saying, "Three is enough! They are too big. People won't finish." I was used to their fights about portion size and cost.

I looked out the plain glass windows and saw a crowd of customers lining up. Fortunately, it didn't include any of my friends. Whenever I went out to eat with people from high school, we went to a *real* restaurant where the waiters were always polite and never kicked anyone out. You couldn't hear the clang of dishes being washed from your seat in the dining room. You didn't have to go outside into an alley to use the bathroom. You didn't have to wait an hour for your food. And when it arrived, it wasn't full of strange flavors, like Mẹ's.

"What do you recommend?" asked a customer, who had just sat down. I heard this a lot, and I often didn't know how to respond. I never told this to customers, but I rarely ate Mẹ's food. I preferred to eat much simpler, blander fare, such as the spaghetti and meat sauce made by Kathy's mother, whom I considered my grandmother. I often suggested the beef with fresh rice noodles because it didn't require a long explanation like so many of Mẹ's other dishes and was so popular. People always enjoyed it.

Tonight, I had a better answer. "Order the curried shrimp and crabmeat," I told him. "The shrimp are huge, practically the size of tennis balls." I knew that the giant shrimp, topped with crabmeat, green onions, and a bright-yellow curry broth, would look gorgeous being carried to a table, and that our customers would "ooh" and "aah" even more than they usually did.

Plus, shrimp and crabmeat were actually high-class, unlike most of the items on Hy Vong's menu. They were foods that might be served at the kind of restaurant I might open if I ever decided to go into the hospitality business. I would open a fancy restaurant that served fancy food. It would definitely have tablecloths. It would be serene and orderly, and the staff would never bicker.

Whatever I was going to do in life, I wanted it to be upper-class. I wanted to dress up in a suit and heels. Preferably, I wanted to work in an office. I wanted to work only on weekdays, not on nights and weekends and holidays like I saw Mẹ and Kathy doing all the time. I wanted to work in a place that was beautiful and polished.

I ended up boxing up a lot of curried shrimp and crabmeat leftovers that night. As usual, Kathy had won the portion-size battle, and most of the customers who ordered it couldn't finish the dish.

Journal entry, age twelve

August 26, 1988

I mean, I love Grandma, Kathy, and Mẹ very much, but why can't I have a normal family? . . . Mẹ thinks I shouldn't be able to spend the night at friends' houses just so I can come home and clean. I mean, be serious! It's just not fair, they're trying to make me grow up before my time. I do have a lot to be thankful for, but nobody I know has to do all the work I do . . . because of all the finance problems we have . . .

And then, Mẹ says, "You will never work as hard as me."

I didn't interact much with Mẹ when I was growing up. She didn't really understand my world. I couldn't talk to her about boys who didn't like me or friendships that had gone awry. She couldn't help me with ballet or homework. Not only had she never experienced these things, we didn't even share enough language to communicate on this level. Our conversations were always simple and in broken English, mainly about what we would be eating that day.

Journal entries, age thirteen

July 6, 1989

Kathy is the only person that I really confide everything in. She's almost like a best friend to me. I love Mẹ because she is my mother. But, when I want someone to tell things to, I go to Kathy.

January 23, 1990

Kathy and I have really worked on me getting stronger. She's gotten me so much exercise equipment, I think we could open our own fitness center . . . all this has really helped. I can do double pirouettes inside to the right, outside both ways. My extensions are a lot higher. I have more control. And, I just plain feel stronger. I wouldn't have been able to make it this far without Kathy behind me. . . . I owe my whole life to her. If it weren't for her, I wouldn't have all the things I have now. I wouldn't even be here. I would be in some bad portion of town, probably.

Kathy opened doors for me that Mẹ would never have known were even there. I might have had to give up on dance if she and her friends hadn't found resources to help me get over the issues with my body and my foot arch. We spent hours driving all over the greater Miami area to find the right pointe shoes that fit my feet. She found Dale, a Pilates instructor, before most people knew Pilates even existed. We drove forty-five minutes each way, twice a week, to go to Pilates class.

I always introduced Kathy as my aunt, yet I considered her one of my parents. Whenever there were parent observation days for ballet, Kathy was always there. Mẹ was never able to come because she was working. When Kathy saw that I was interested in science, she asked around and someone told her about a special program where I could do neuroscience research in university science labs, after school.

Even though we never seemed to have much money, Kathy was always taking us on big trips to see iconic American sights. When I was little, we traveled to New York City, and she watched me while she sent Mẹ on a tour of the United Nations. That backfired—Mẹ didn't understand a word and glared at Kathy each time the tour group passed us! But Kathy was unfazed, and as I grew older, she regularly convinced Mẹ to close the restaurant for a few days each year so we could go on the road.

Kathy learned that we could collect S&H green stamps in a supermarket rewards program to trade in for a tent and other camping equipment. We drove up Route 1 in California, visiting national parks and vineyards, sometimes sleeping on a beach for

159

free. We hiked along the Appalachian Trail. We spent the Fourth of July in Washington D.C. We even drove to Disney World in our home state a few times; Mẹ particularly enjoyed the Japan- and China-themed acrobatic performances.

When things got really tense with Mẹ's marriage to Bao, Kathy took me camping in the Everglades for a weekend, where we saw the sun rise and watched the stars. For a few days, we forgot all about everything back home.

Journal entry, age fourteen

August 5, 1991

Right now Duc is giving Kathy this big speech about how Mẹ is not good and doesn't understand him. . . . Now he's saying that I should be "Vietnamese." He's saying that I should have a Vietnamese father and mother . . . he makes me so disgusted.

Mẹ told me very little about her childhood, and almost nothing about her journey to the United States. Once I was in school, speaking English, she didn't try to make me speak Vietnamese at home, and she never tried to send me to a Vietnamese school. We rarely socialized with other Vietnamese families or went to Vietnamese cultural events. The closest thing I ever got to a cultural lesson was going shopping at Asian grocery stores for food that I then refused to eat.

My friends were all from school or ballet—only a few were Asian, and none was Vietnamese. Other than Mẹ, the only Vietnamese people I came into close contact with were Bao and Duc, neither of whom I liked or respected.

Many years later, I realized why Mẹ had not immersed me more in Vietnamese culture: She viewed that culture as quicksand. She had to earn every opportunity one painful inch at a time, often defying her own family—and even then, she found that other Vietnamese would not acknowledge her hard-fought progress. They would see only that she was poor and from the country and continue to regard her as a servant.

So when she arrived in the United States and saw that American children had more opportunities, she wanted me to be a part of that culture. Not the one that made her feel trapped, like she could never get anywhere no matter how hard she tried.

As a teenager, I didn't know any of this. I just knew that I could communicate with her on only the most basic levels. Sometimes I wished that she would work less, so that I could see her more.

As for my lack of a father? I rarely thought about it. It wasn't like his absence changed who I was or what I was doing. I didn't have an incomplete family. I just had a very different kind of family.

Journal entry, age sixteen

June 9, 1993
Mẹ and Kathy have already said they are more than willing to pay for college. The point is that I refuse to let them. After high school, I'm going to try to become as independent as possible.

I came to look at college from a purely practical standpoint. I regarded the situation exactly as I think Mẹ would have approached it—had she even known what college was, which she didn't. We never discussed college at home. We never sat around the dining room table and reviewed college applications, compared college brochures, or discussed what made a student qualified for specific schools. What I knew about college came from my advisors at my public school and my friends, many of whom were planning to attend the University of Miami and other state schools.

I knew my family didn't have much money, and no one told me about the financial aid system. I just knew that if I attended a local state school, it would cost my family the least amount of money.

When it came time to apply to colleges, Kathy asked my advisors for suggestions. "Look," one counselor told her. "She's never going to get into a top college, so don't even bother applying."

This advice made practical sense to me, and besides, it would be the least expensive option. If someone who was an expert in college applications thought I wouldn't get into a top college, then I figured he was probably right. How was I supposed to know any better?

But unlike Mẹ and me, Kathy had never been practical. She always resisted the instructions of others. She never thought rationally about what to do. Instead, she believed in going big and always told me to follow my dreams. And she always found a way so that I could do what I wanted to do, even if others, such as my ballet teacher, told me I couldn't.

So after Kathy heard my counselor's advice, she decided to hurl his words right out the window.

"Apply to Harvard," she suggested.

"Harvard?" I responded. That had never occurred to me.

"Why not?" she said. "It's the number one school in America. You have good grades, you have ballet, you've tutored children, you've worked in science labs. You've even won national science awards. Apply to some Ivy League schools. The worst thing that's going to happen is that you won't get in."

"Harvard is expensive," I said.

Kathy shook her head. "Don't limit yourself. Go as high as you can. Tung and I will figure out how to pay for it."

I was doubtful, but I filled out the lengthy Ivy League applications.

A few months later, I looked in disbelief at an acceptance letter from Harvard.

Kathy wasn't surprised at all. She was only ecstatic because she believed all along that this letter would come. When we told Mẹ, she burst out of the kitchen with tears of joy streaming down her face. She wrapped me in a long, fierce hug. "I'm so proud of you," she said.

To my further surprise, my worries about money were quickly resolved. Harvard awarded me a full scholarship, including room and board. We would need to pay only for books and extra living costs.

I knew my acceptance to Harvard would give Mẹ and Kathy major bragging rights. The pride was mounting in me, too. Of course, I was proud that I could attend a school with such a prestigious academic reputation. I was also thrilled to be heading to such a majestic campus. I imagined getting lost in libraries so big you couldn't see the ends of the rows of books. When I visited Harvard and walked among the historical stone-and-brick buildings and expansive green lawns, I felt an exhilaration that I had never known before. I felt like I could do anything. I could be anyone.

Kathy and Mẹ closed Hy Vong for one night so they could attend my high school graduation ceremony. Kathy put this sign in the window that paid tribute to Mẹ's humble roots: "Our daughter is the first in the family to graduate from high school—God Bless America!"

The biggest shrimp. The best college. The most outlandish, impractical dreams. Kathy believed we should all have them—and sometimes we could.

Curried Shrimp and Crabmeat

This luxurious, warmly spiced dish can be made without crab, if you prefer. We recommend using heavy cream. You can use coconut milk if you like, but it curdles when you add it to a hot curry. You must first cool the curry until it's lukewarm (about 30 minutes), add the coconut milk, then slowly reheat the dish.

MAKES 4 OR 5 GENEROUS MAIN-COURSE SERVINGS

3 Tbsp vegetable oil

½ small sweet onion, chopped

1½ tsp curry powder

2½ lb [1.2 kg] jumbo shrimp (preferably U-10 size, meaning 10 shrimp per 1 lb [455 g], or bigger), peeled, butterflied, and deveined, leaving any orange roe

½ stalk of lemongrass, white part only, thinly sliced (discard tough outer layers)

2¾ cups [660 ml] Hy Vong Stock (page 66), hot or warm

2 Tbsp plus ¾ tsp fish sauce

1¼ tsp kosher salt

¼ tsp black pepper

¼ tsp Accent Flavor Enhancer (optional)

8 oz [230 g] cooked jumbo lump crabmeat

¼ cup [60 ml] heavy cream or coconut milk

4 to 5 cups [480 to 600 g] cooked jasmine rice, for serving

5 green onions, green parts only, sliced, for garnish

In a large pot, heat the oil over high heat. Add half of the sweet onion and cook, stirring occasionally, until lightly browned, about 2 minutes. Stir in the curry powder, then lower the heat to medium-high and add the shrimp, remaining sweet onion, the lemongrass, 2 cups [480 ml] of the stock, 2 Tbsp plus ¼ tsp of the fish sauce, 1 tsp of the salt, the pepper, and Accent (if using). Cook without stirring until the shrimp are just cooked through, 5 to 7 minutes (fewer if you are using smaller shrimp).

Meanwhile, in a small saucepan, heat the crabmeat and remaining ¾ cup [180 ml] stock over medium-high heat, stirring gently, until the liquid boils and the crabmeat is heated through, about 5 minutes. Remove from the heat, add the remaining ¼ tsp salt and ½ tsp fish sauce, and gently combine. Add the crab mixture to the shrimp. Let cool slightly, then gently stir in the cream. Serve with rice and top with the green onions.

CHAPTER 13

Leaving

Miami, 1993 to 1994

TUNG:

I felt a lightness that I had never known before. My daughter was going to Harvard. Everyone said Harvard was the best school in America. The very best! As soon as I heard the news, I stopped feeling tired. My eyes opened wider, my shoulders loosened. I was like a flower opening up its petals. I no longer felt the burden of the countless days cutting onions and ginger alone, or the loneliness from not understanding this strange country where I had worked so hard to raise Phuong Lien.

Finally, I belonged. I belonged in America. Not only that, but now I belonged in the Vietnamese community, too. My daughter going to Harvard had raised my status so high, higher than anyone in my family had ever known—higher than I could have ever dreamed.

To celebrate Phuong Lien's high school graduation, we discussed going back to Vietnam to see my family. I was still ashamed about leaving them, but now I felt that shame beginning to lift. I felt like my journey to America had all worked out.

But there were still dark memories of my journey here that I had been keeping buried for years. Avoiding them became much easier after I had a child and opened the restaurant, which took up all my time and energy. Maybe it was time to face what had happened during my last hours in Saigon. As we prepared for our trip, I also prepared to explain the story to my family. I had to remember everything I had tried so hard to forget.

Saigon, April 1975

The morning started like any other day. I woke up early, climbed aboard a rickshaw, and rode through the streets of Saigon to go to the butcher. I brought my pail of bones back to the market and turned them into soup. After we opened, Sinh waited on customers in the front, while I prepared the food in the back.

Suddenly, Sinh came to me in a panic. "People are running," she said, panting. "I don't know why. Everyone is running."

I looked out from behind my pot and my heart began to pound. I saw chaos. Shoving. Screaming. Arms waving. Terrified faces. What was happening? We saw an older woman we knew, Bà Bai. "Why are you sitting here?" she said. "You should run! The Viet Cong are coming!"

I shook and took short, quick breaths as Bà Bai kept talking. So many words: *Communist. Army. They will take women. Hostages. Prizes for soldiers who had no arms or legs. That will be you. Go now!*

I barely heard the words, but I understood the danger. If we did not run, we could become slaves. I tried to move, but almost collapsed.

"I can't run!" I said. "I have to go home."

My mother. Her brick house. Điện Bàn. Safety.

"How will you go home?" asked Bà Bai. "No planes. No buses. No trains."

167

"Really?" I said. My heart was beating louder than the screaming around us. "My God."

I looked at Sinh. Her hands covered her mouth. "Sinh. What do we do?"

"Oh my God," Sinh managed to say. "We're dead. Dead."

"Bà Bai, are you going to run?" I asked.

Bà Bai shook her head. "I'm too old. I'm staying. You're young. You go."

"Where do I go?"

"A lot of people are going to boats," Bà Bai said, pointing in the direction of the river. "From there to the mountains. They wait for the soldiers to leave. They eat packaged noodles and bananas."

She gave us a gentle push. "You go, too. You are young. The Communists will take you."

The yelling in the market grew deafening. I tried to think. Should we pack? Should we take our pot and spoon? On the way to our rented room, we heard a man yell, "The Viet Cong are at Biên Hòa!" That was near my butcher. So close.

We burst our door open. We tossed pants, shirts in a bag. My grandmother's ruby ring was already in my pocket. We ran back out the door, my left hand gripping Sinh's right hand.

"The river!" I screamed. My legs pounded the sidewalk. Streets flew by.

"I lost a shoe!" cried Sinh.

"Keep running!" I yelled.

Water, up ahead. A boat filled with screaming people. A boat about to push away. A man, unwinding a rope from the pier.

"Oh my God! Sinh, jump!" I yelled. We had to get on this boat. *We could not become slaves.* The man had a stick. He pushed away from the pier. *We could not become slaves.* I flung my body at the boat.

My right foot made it over the side. Two strong arms grabbed my right arm. A man pulled me in. My back slammed into the bottom of the boat.

My left hand was empty.

Sinh! I reached out and raised my head to see out of the boat.

Water. Sinh. Black hair swirling. Sinh, sinking.

"SINH!" I screamed, reaching out my hand to her again. I could only watch as her body sank deeper into the river, becoming smaller and smaller, until I could see nothing at all.

+ + +

Eventually, I managed to loosen my grip on the edge of the boat and elbow enough people so that I had room to sit down. I wiped my tears and looked around the wooden vessel, where I now sat, shoulder to shoulder, with about 120 people on the upper deck. Men. Women. A few children. A man steered the boat from the front near where I had landed. Another man stood at the back by a motor that I could hear humming.

I did not speak to anyone. I did not know who pulled me into the boat. I did not know where we were going. I assumed we were headed to the mountains to eat packaged noodles until the Communists—whoever they were—were gone. Where were the mountains? Only water lay ahead.

Surely, we would be there soon. Hours went by, with only dark blue ocean as far as I could see. The owner of the boat handed out plastic cups of water once, and then the water was gone. Then darkness started to fall.

Bà Bai was lying. No mountains. No food. No way to see my family, or to tell Sinh's family what had happened to her. My tongue scratched the roof of my dry mouth. My vision started to blur. Hours and then days began to melt together into a mess of sensations, sounds, and sights.

Dark storm clouds covered the sky. The narrow boat pitched in the waves. People yelled as the storm began: "Go back! Go back!" Rain poured onto my face, and I parted my dry lips in relief, eagerly drinking what I could. The stench of urine and vomit filled my nose as seasickness consumed us. I did not move. If I did, I would lose my seat.

The clouds parted. The ocean shone, beautiful and calm. Whales or dolphins jumped near the horizon. Children moaned. The owners of the boat used their radio to try to call for a big ship. Blackness fell. I drifted in and out of dreams under the light of a half-moon and a sky filled with stars.

Faces fell slack and still. Older people. Children. I thought of Sinh, sinking into the river. I dreamed of the worried faces of Sinh's parents, of my mother, brothers, and sister. I thought of the families of the people dying around me. They would never know that the people had died in a boat, and that their bodies had been thrown overboard into the ocean. They would never know that their death came as a relief to those of us who now had more room to sit.

I spoke to Trời, to the spirits of Bà Nội and my father. *Help me. Save me. Help me get to land, so I can help my family. If I die, I can't help my family.*

More rain poured on my face. I drank. My lips cracked and bled. I dreamed about home, fishing, farming. My stomach rumbled as I thought of the taste of fish and vegetables, the meaty scent of bún bò huế.

I spoke to myself. *I am a water lily.* These flowers grew atop the waters of Điện Bàn. The little pops of beauty, pink and purple, did not sink. Instead, they floated along with the ripples of water. When I was growing up, I always tried to spot the delicate stalks because they meant a meal: they were often a hiding place for fish.

Now, rocking back and forth in this boat, I, too, floated atop the water, floated wherever the waves took me. When I hit the ground, wherever that ground was, I would plant roots.

+ + +

Yelling. "Oh my God!"

We had been floating for about nine days, with nothing in sight except for ocean. Now, a large gray ship loomed in the distance. With our last bit of energy, we scrambled to our feet and waved our hands in the air. I thanked Trời. Then I noticed one woman who was still sitting. Her hands clutched her stomach. Fluid soaked her pants. She moaned long and loud.

I recognized that moan. I had seen a few births in my village. People began backing away from her, shooting glares at her. "Go downstairs," a man told her. Others ignored her. Not me. "We need to help her," I said. "Can anyone help her?" No one volunteered.

I made my way over to her, took her arm, and pulled her to a standing position. Slowly we walked to the stairs, and I helped her down into the now-empty dim lower deck. The woman looked around at the dirty engine pieces scattered around and eased herself onto a board on the floor.

"Did your husband come with you? Your family?" I asked.

She shook her head.

"Then why did you go?" I asked.

"Everybody told me, run!" she said, wincing as she spoke. "So I ran."

She moaned. I took her hand. When I saw her baby's head come out, I cradled it gently and helped support the body as it followed. It was a boy. He was covered in blood, but thankfully I could hear little whimpers. I took one of my spare shirts from my bag and wiped the blood out of his eyes as best as I could. I wiped his cheeks and forehead. Then I wrapped my shirt around him and handed him to his mother.

I knew that I was supposed to cut the cord, but I did not see a knife. So, I took a sharp engine part and split the cord, then tied a knot.

"Chị," I said to the mother, using the familial Vietnamese word for sister. "We have to go back upstairs." She was smiling through her terror at the baby, who had started to cry, softly. This woman was so weak. How could I get her upstairs so we would all be rescued? I gave the woman one pair of my pants. They just barely fit around her. I took the baby and motioned that we should start climbing up the ladder. We went very slowly, with me leading the way. "Thank you," the woman said with every step. "Thank you."

When I got to the top, I hoisted the baby and myself onto the deck. It was empty. Everyone was gone. The blood drained from my face. We had missed the rescue! I whirled around, and fortunately, I saw that the ship was still nearby.

I gave the baby to his mother and dropped my bag. I raised both arms, waving frantically to the sailors onboard. I nearly collapsed in relief when they waved back. One got into a big net. A crane lowered him and the net onto our much smaller boat. The sailor was a tall man wearing an olive green uniform, brown hair peeking out from his white hat. He helped me inside the net, and we rose high above my home for the past nine days.

The sailor set me on the deck of the rescue ship. I watched him get back into the net and return to rescue the mother and her baby. Another sailor handed me a red can. "Coke," he said. I took a drink of the dark fluid. I had never tasted such overwhelming sweetness. Even though I had had only a little water and no food since leaving Saigon, I put the can down. He tried bottles of water next. I drank five in a row.

I could barely remember who I was. But, thank Trời, I was alive, and I would eventually be taken to a refugee camp in Guam, then flown to America. The water lily had landed at last.

CHAPTER 14

Vietnam

Vietnam, 1993 to 1994

TUNG:

I had carried so much guilt for so long. After I finally made contact with my family in 1985, I started sending money: $100 here, $100 there, whatever I could manage. I wanted to visit them, but at the time the United States did not allow travel to Vietnam. Hoping that one day the laws would change, I socked away my spare change. Each time I put a few quarters into the jar, I thought about seeing my mother's face again.

In 1991, Kathy read in the newspaper that the United States had lifted its travel restrictions against Vietnam. By then I was making a $500-a-week salary at Hy Vong. Realizing that visiting my family was actually possible now, I spent even less so I could save even more. Holes started to appear in my clothes, but what did that matter?

By the time Phuong Lien's high school graduation approached, I had saved enough for the three of us to make the trip. Our tickets and visas cost $7,000. That left me with about $6,000 to buy gifts for my family, including my mother, my siblings, their spouses, and all of their children. I thought about what they might need. I bought ten suitcases and packed them full of clothes and luxuries I knew would be scarce in Điện Bàn, such as aspirin, vitamins, toothpaste, toothbrushes, and soap. I made sure to include twenty-four bottles of Eagle Brand Medicated Oil, a green menthol-based substance. It was a precious treasure in the village, one of the few medications they had. You smelled it to relieve headaches and rubbed it on sore muscles for relief.

We left Miami in December 1993. It took three days and four different airports to reach Đà Nẵng. When I walked out of customs, I looked through the glass doors and saw my mother standing in the middle of a group of her grandchildren.

She looked so old. So skinny. So tired. Our eyes locked, and I started to cry. How had she survived all of these years while I was away? How did she take care of all of these children? How had she kept the family together? As soon as I reached her, my mother grabbed me into a hug. My brother Lai came up from behind her. The three of us held each other and cried. "I'm sorry," I choked through my tears.

Almost two decades had passed since we last saw each other. I wanted to know everything. I had so many questions. To my disappointment, my mother was mostly silent during the taxi ride to our hotel in Đà Nẵng. She spoke only with her eyes: They searched my face, looked at my clothes.

When we reached the hotel, we learned that the government would not permit us to travel to Điện Bàn. We decided that my mother would stay at our hotel with us. I would share a room with her. Once we were alone, my mother spoke.

"Where is your grandmother's ring?" she asked me.

I smiled and asked, "Why? Do you think I would sell it?" I tapped my purse. "I have it." I brought out the sparkling ring to show her.

My mother looked at the large pink stone. She nodded. "Good. I'm glad you didn't sell it."

I shook my head. "Sometimes I needed money," I admitted, "but I was never going to sell it."

She nodded.

My mother had never slept on a mattress before. In Điện Bàn, everyone slept on mats and cots. We shared the soft bed in my room. Our eyes closed quickly that first night, our bodies and minds drained from the travel and reunion.

I woke up around midnight; the room was silent and dark. Jet lag had set in, but also a desperation to connect—really connect—with my mother. Maybe she would open up when it was dark and everyone else was sleeping. I rocked her bony shoulder, nudging her out of her sleep. She opened her eyes and looked at me. Softly, I asked her what I had spent years wondering.

"How did you take care of the children? What did you do?"

My mother rubbed her eyes, then said, "I took it one day at a time." She said that she had help from my father's brother, the same uncle who had traveled to Saigon to bring back my money.

When the war ended and the Communists began to take over the land people farmed, my mother feared that my three teenage brothers would be forced to join the North Vietnamese Army. She turned to her secret weapon: Mau, my blind younger brother. Unlike mine, his singing voice was beautiful, the most beautiful in the village. So when the Communists came, my mother told Mau, "Sing for them."

He did. During their breaks, Mau sang North Vietnamese songs, which they loved. The plan worked: The soldiers left my brothers alone and allowed my family to work on their land, which was now the government-run farms. My two youngest brothers, Thuong and Lai, later agreed to fight for the Vietnamese military in Cambodia. Thankfully, both returned safely. That was all my mother would tell me that first night. She wanted to listen to me talk.

"What is America like?" she asked.

"Trời sent me to the right place," I said. I told her that I had Kathy and Kathy's mother, a place to stay, and a place for my daughter to grow. I even had a restaurant, where I cooked. I made sure she understood that I cooked a lot, and I cooked well. Really, really well.

"How did you take care of Phuong Lien?" she asked. I told her about raising Phuong Lien and how much Kathy—and later, her mother—helped me. When I mentioned that I sewed all of her dresses from small pieces of material that I had found on sale, my mother's mouth dropped open.

"You sew?" she asked.

"I know, I never knew how to sew," I told her. "When I went to America, I had to think about how to do a lot of things. I had to sew. So I did."

My mother looked at me with pride. "Your Bà Nội was right," she said. "She always said, 'Don't worry about Tung.'"

We were quiet for a few minutes, remembering Bà Nội.

"Is America beautiful?" my mother asked.

"Yes," I answered. "Someday you should go there with me. I will take you around and show you."

She did not reply.

In the morning, I went to the hotel restaurant and bought my mother a Coke so that she could taste what I drank after I was rescued. We drove around Đà Nẵng. Everything was so different. There were more buildings. It was louder and more crowded. We crossed a river to go to my brother Kiem's house, just outside Điện Bàn.

That was as far as the government would allow Kathy, Phuong Lien, and me to go, although they didn't give us a reason for the restrictions. I could see that the road between Đà Nẵng and Điện Bàn had grown wider and was so much busier. I barely recognized the spot by the side of the road where I had sold bún bò huế all those years ago.

When I saw my brother's house, made of rice-paddy stalks, I knew I had to help my family even more. I didn't want them living in that kind of house. "I will send money," I offered, "to build better houses." Everyone got excited and wanted one. I told them I would have to send money slowly. "I am only one me in America, and I still need to take care of Phuong Lien."

Each house would cost about $1,500 in U.S. dollars to build. I thought I could manage to send enough money for one house a year. I would start with my mother. She needed a house that was farther away from the river. The last one I built her flooded every time it rained.

My youngest siblings, now adults themselves, peered curiously at me as we talked. They were so little the last time they saw me that they only knew me from the stories my mother told them and from the faded photo of me when I was a young child.

My mother instructed everyone to say, "Thank you, Chị Hai."

Chị Hai. Oldest sister.

The last person who had called me that was Sinh.

Later, when we were alone again, I explained to my mother what had happened to Sinh and asked her to tell Sinh's family. I also gave her the last bit of my savings, $500, to give to them. "Please tell them I am sorry. I let go of Sinh and she sank into the river." After a few moments, I gently added, "Please don't cry."

What I didn't share with my mother was that I often wondered if Sinh might have survived if we had been running from something in America. Americans always seemed to help each other and care about each other. Aside from the people who told us the Communists were coming and who had helped me into the boat, I did not feel that Vietnamese people were the same. In Vietnam, we were all on our own.

I was happy to see my family. But I missed America.

KATHY:

Tung's family didn't know what to make of me.

"Do you have a husband?" they asked.

I just laughed. "Americans always ask me the same thing!" I replied in the Vietnamese I had learned over the years.

I watched as Tung gave out her gifts. As I thought of the sacrifices she had made to save money, Tung's family snatched them up without so much as a thank-you. Phuongy and I watched as they dove over each other to take as many of the sweatshirts, toothbrushes, and medicine bottles as they could, not making any effort to share equally.

However, my biggest surprise in Vietnam was that the food was nowhere near as good as what we served at Hy Vong. I had been looking forward to mouthwatering stir-fries and complex soups. Yet no matter what we ate, I spent each meal thinking that Tung could have made it better. Each soup was blander and thinner than Tung's. We ate so much barbecued pork, and it was always drier and less flavorful. Tung just put so much care into her cooking, and she had an innate sense of seasoning. I ate well enough through Vietnam but couldn't wait to get home to Tung's food.

+ + +

Over the next five years, Tung sent home a total of $6,000, enough for four houses. We got to see them when we returned to Vietnam in 1999, this time without Phuongy.

By the time we made this visit, the government had relaxed its rules and allowed us to stay in Điện Bàn with Tung's family for the entire three weeks. An official told me that I was the first American to ever stay overnight in the village, where the living conditions were still very primitive. I was excited to return to my Girl Scout days of boiling water over a campfire and sleeping on a cot. Tung, on the other hand, had become so Americanized that shortly before we arrived, she sent her family a mini water heater so she could have hot showers.

When Tung's mother saw me, she let loose a torrent of Vietnamese: "Khi nào bà Mỹ đi." She didn't realize that I spoke a lot of Vietnamese by then and knew she was asking, "When will the American woman go?" I thought to myself, *I better become friends with her. Here I am in the middle of the country with nowhere else to go.*

The Điện Bàn landscape was acres and acres of rice fields. I didn't know east from west. One day, I was outside looking around while Tung was talking with her mother in the house. A couple of Tung's brothers tapped me on my arm and motioned that I should follow them, so I did.

We walked for a few minutes until we reached a group of men sitting on folding chairs, whom I quickly realized were the village leaders. They pointed at an empty chair for me to sit on. "Why are you visiting with a Vietnamese?" they asked.

I responded in Vietnamese: "We are here to see her family." And that was it. Tung's brothers and I returned to the house.

But two days later, they brought me back to the village leaders, who again asked, "Why are you visiting with a Vietnamese?" I gave them the same answer.

That happened a few more times during my stay. I eventually got used to the routine. The leaders, having lived through the war, could not understand how an American and a Vietnamese could be friends.

It reminded me of how some members of my family had been skeptical of Tung and had such a hard time viewing us as a family. And of how Tung's mother would have preferred her daughter to come home without me. By now, Tung and I didn't even see each other as Vietnamese or as American. We were just friends, and a team, who had accepted each other long ago and worked together for so many years.

During another lazy afternoon, as I watched some of Tung's nieces and nephews playing soccer, a group of Vietnamese teenagers came up to me, waving silver dog tags. They instantly reminded me of the dog tags that my mother had made me wear as a child in Iowa in case I got lost. "Oh, the kids have those in America," I told them, cheerfully. "I wore one."

When they kept dangling them in front of me, I got confused and said I didn't know what they wanted. Then I saw a group of men standing behind the kids, goading them on. I assumed that they gave the kids the tags. One of them finally commented before they left me alone: "She knows, but she's not talking."

It wasn't until later that I realized my ignorance helped me dodge what could have been a really uncomfortable situation. The men probably pulled those dog tags off of a dead soldier during the war, and they were essentially using the kids to confront me about the Americans' role in the war, and maybe even their own personal losses.

Meanwhile, Tung's family seemed to have figured out that they weren't getting rid of me anytime soon, so they started cooking elaborate feasts for us—with Tung's help. They would spend the whole day cooking, and at night we would sit on the floor around a blanket covered with the dishes, which included boiled quail eggs, asparagus and crab soup, and, of course, bún bò huế.

My favorite food discovery during all of those meals happened to be the most humble. Mắm tôm, a fermented shrimp paste, had been a staple of Tung's childhood and sometimes the only thing they had to eat. It consists of baby shrimp gathered from local streams that are ground raw, fermented, then mixed with lime juice, garlic, and salt. We regularly bought and cooked with mắm (as I called it) in America, but that jarred version didn't compare to this fresh one. I couldn't get enough of its pungent tartness.

+++

Tung and I would eventually return to Vietnam a third time, in 2002. We wanted to bring Tung's teenage niece back to Miami to work with us. Tung had a hard time finding anyone who would make food to her standards in Hy Vong's kitchen, so we thought it made sense to tap a Vietnamese relative. Due to some red tape, it didn't end up happening, but while we tried to sort it out, we got to spend a lot of time in Saigon. Although it was now technically called Ho Chi Minh City, we never used that name.

We stayed at the lovely Renaissance Riverside Hotel. Although I firmly believe that fancy hotels are not the way to learn about what Vietnam is really like, this one was convenient to the many government agencies we had to visit, and we wanted Tung's niece to experience an urban setting.

The hotel sat right on the Saigon River, the same body of water that had carried Tung out of Vietnam almost thirty years earlier. Each morning we sat in an ornate dining room and feasted on the big buffet—eggs every style, beautiful bowls of phở, lush chunks of dragon fruit.

As we ate, we looked out the window onto a lively part of the city. We saw people balancing large piles of ice and other goods on their bicycles, motorbikes zooming by, and professionals walking to work. I noticed Tung's eyes land on a lone woman by the river. She carried a pole across her shoulders, baskets hanging from either end. A pot was visible in one of them.

I wondered what Tung was thinking as she watched the soup merchant walking around in search of a customer. I wondered if she had been transported back to her past.

That's when Tung turned to me and said, "This is like Disney World."

Barbecued Pork with Rice Noodles (Bún Thịt Nướng)

At Hy Vong, our landlord hated the smell of burning charcoal, so we always waited until he went home each day, around four in the afternoon, to fire up the grill. You, too, will get the best flavor by grilling the meat over charcoal, but feel free to use a gas grill if that's what you have.

We consider a grill basket essential to creating the moistest pork possible, and the key is not to place the basket right on top of the grill. Instead, place a 2 in [5 cm] high clean stone on top of the grill, rest an edge of the grill basket on the stone, and rotate the basket frequently. If you can't find a stone of this height, a heatproof ramekin, an inverted baking dish, or a foil-covered brick are all good substitutes. We promise the extra attention will pay off.

SERVES 6

3¾ lb [1.7 kg] boneless pork butt, or that amount of meat cut off a bone-in pork butt, trimmed of most of the fat and cut against the grain into thin, 3 in [7.5 cm] long slices

2 stalks of lemongrass, white part only, thinly sliced (discard tough outer layers)

6 green onions, white and very light green parts only

4 large garlic cloves

¾ cup [105 g] untoasted white sesame seeds

¼ cup [60 ml] fish sauce

2 Tbsp lime juice

1 Tbsp vegetable oil

1 Tbsp sugar

1 Tbsp kosher salt

1 tsp black pepper

1 tsp Accent Flavor Enhancer (optional)

2 cups [about 200 g] bean sprouts

1½ lb [680 g] rice vermicelli (bún), prepared according to the package directions

4 carrots, grated

1 bunch mint, leaves chopped

1 bunch cilantro, leaves chopped

1 bunch basil, leaves chopped

1½ cups [210 g] crushed, finely chopped, or ground dry-roasted unsalted peanuts

3 cups [720 ml] Nước Chấm (page 105), warmed

Put the pork in a large bowl and set aside. In the bowl of a food processor, pulse the lemongrass several times until chopped. Add the green onions and garlic and pulse until finely chopped. Scrape the mixture over the pork, then add the sesame seeds, fish sauce, lime juice, vegetable oil, sugar, salt, pepper, and Accent (if using). Mix thoroughly with your hands, then let marinate at room temperature for 10 to 20 minutes.

Meanwhile, prepare a charcoal or gas grill. Arrange the pork in a grill basket in a double layer.

Put a clean 2 in [5 cm] high stone (or one of the substitutes mentioned in the headnote) on top of the grill's grate. Rest an edge of the basket on the stone so that the meat cooks slowly. Cook, turning the basket every few minutes, until the pork is deeply browned, 15 to 20 minutes.

Divide the bean sprouts, lightly crushing them with your hands, among six bowls. Top with the noodles, followed by the carrots, mint, cilantro, basil, peanuts, and pork. Pour ½ cup [120 ml] of the nước chấm over each bowl or serve it on the side. The traditional way to eat this dish is to mix up all the ingredients in your bowl, but feel free to do as you like.

CHAPTER 15

Independence

Cambridge, MA, and Miami, 1994 to 1998

TUNG:

I had never seen so many bricks!

The buildings of Harvard University seemed to reach into the sky. I gazed at the rows and rows of red bricks that stretched up into grand towers and turrets. I thought back to the years in Điện Bàn when I made bricks, one by one, throwing clay deep into the molds, dragging a pile home every night, to make a one-room house for my parents. How had Americans made these huge brick buildings, and how long must they have taken to build?

"This is an amazing school," I said to Kathy.

Kathy smiled. "This is *Harvard!*" she exclaimed.

After we moved Phuong Lien into her dorm room, I walked through the campus feeling like, finally, I was walking through air, instead of dragging my feet through quicksand. I thought about how my daughter was an adult now. She had seen where I came from. I could share more with her, more about my life. When she was a child, I just wanted her to be happy. I protected her from anything that would make her sad. Now I didn't have to protect her from things that might be painful. Of course, I still wanted her to be happy.

After Kathy and I flew back to Miami, I thought a lot about what my daughter must be eating at college. She didn't like most of my food, but she did like the American food that Kathy's mother made. I thought that maybe I should try to make American food, too. I could serve it to her when she came to visit. Maybe that was one way I could connect with her now that she was so far away.

I had seen many people in America eat macaroni and cheese. I thought it was an unusual dish because it did not contain meat or vegetables. It also seemed so bland. How could I make macaroni and cheese that had more flavor?

Meat, I decided. On my next day off from the restaurant, I stood barefoot in our home kitchen and pulled my hair back with a headband. I chopped some onion and garlic, sautéed that with ground beef, and added a bit of fish sauce and Accent seasoning. Once that was done, I mixed it with cooked macaroni and poured everything into a pan. I had purchased a bag of Colby-Jack, Colby and Monterey Jack cheeses already conveniently shredded and combined in a plastic package. All I had to do was sprinkle it over the top. Americans made some things so complicated but other things so easy.

LYN:

Journal entry, age seventeen, written right after returning from Vietnam

January 2, 1993

I think about Mẹ's family and how they can't do a lot. It is because they have never had the chance. But the weird thing is that Mẹ could do all of these things these people can't. Why? She can sew. She can farm and be very productive. She went out and sold soup

185

on the streets. She went to Saigon to open a restaurant. Why can't they? I have a feeling they don't have the driving force she has.

Mẹ and I have become relatively close in the last few days. . . . She and I have really talked. Sometimes I really wish she didn't have to work so hard so that I could see her more. Oh well. Maybe soon. I hope they start making some changes, because time isn't standing still or going backwards.

Something in Mẹ changed after we returned from our first trip to Vietnam, right before my high school graduation. It became particularly obvious after I left home for Harvard.

For one thing, she started talking.

When I called home to say hello, I expected to exchange greetings with Mẹ and then talk to Kathy. But instead, Mẹ would talk on and on about what happened that day, what happened at the restaurant. She wanted to know all about my day, and she wanted to know more than my previous stock answers that it was "fun" or "great." She began to ask questions about what I was studying, what activities I was enjoying.

Though we now lived apart for the first time, we were talking more than we ever had before. We had long conversations over the phone about the friends I was making, the classes I was choosing. I even told her about organizing a Model United Nations event in Budapest, which had turned into a complicated struggle to find cheap housing for students from all over the world. She listened with great interest.

On one of my visits home, I stopped by Hy Vong and saw customers go to the kitchen window and say, "Hi, Tung! Dinner was delicious! I am so full!" I expected Mẹ to give them her usual smile and nod, and for them to go on their way.

Instead, she paused her stirring. "What did you eat?" she asked them. "Did you have enough to eat?" "See you next week!"

I was floored. I had never seen her so social and comfortable with customers.

I was even more surprised when we sat down to dinner at home later that week, and Mẹ continued her banter. She told us how many pounds of soursop fruit she had harvested from her tree. She wanted to discuss what customer had gotten married recently, which was normally the sort of topic that would interest only Kathy. What used to be a short dinner turned into hours of Kathy, Mẹ, and me talking and eating a dish I would have never expected.

I was bewildered when she set down a pan of baked macaroni and cheese. I had never seen her cook American food. When we ate American food at home, it was because my grandmother—Kathy's mother—had cooked it. She also rarely used processed ingredients, such as pre-shredded cheese. When I took a bite, not only was it some of the best macaroni and cheese I had ever eaten, but I realized that she had made it her own.

Mẹ was trying Italian-American dishes, too, such as spaghetti with unusually light meatballs that she slowly simmered in chicken stock. She made lasagna, layered with long, thin slices of the bright-green-skinned squash that she grew in the backyard. She told me that she assumed those were the types of foods they served in the Harvard cafeteria, where I had a meal plan. She was so proud of the dishes, and I was touched that she made them for me. I hadn't told her yet what else I was eating at Harvard.

A couple times a month, I ventured away from campus and rode the "T"—Boston's subway—to a small Vietnamese restaurant in Boston's Chinatown. It had bare walls, tacky decorations, and unadorned windows that all reminded me of Hy Vong. I sat on a plastic chair, ordered from a plastic-covered menu, and ate phở out of a plastic bowl.

I had rarely chosen to eat Vietnamese food when I was growing up. Suddenly, 1,500 miles [2,400 km] from home, I craved its flavors, smells, textures, and familiarity. Maybe it was part of my adjustment to New England culture, which I hadn't realized would be so much more proper and formal than Miami's.

+ + +

The biggest shock of my college years was learning the depth of Mẹ's frustration with Kathy. As Mẹ and I began really connecting and sharing details about our lives, she began to open up in ways I didn't expect: "Hy Vong is so busy, but I never see money," she confided. "Kathy just spends money like it is water. I work so hard and Kathy gives away food."

On our next call, she brought it up again, "Kathy is stupid! We never have enough money! I am so tired. I work day and night and I don't see the money."

I was having so much fun finally learning about Mẹ, but that joy was tempered by how frustrated she had become. As we talked more, I began to realize that a lot of her frustration came from not having the language to communicate. She didn't know how to speak English very well, and she had also lost a lot of her Vietnamese language.

That impacted her life in several ways. First, it meant that Mẹ couldn't handle the business aspects of Hy Vong. She had to leave all of the buying and paying the bills to Kathy. Kathy didn't care about the bottom line: She just wanted everyone to be happy. She made very different choices than Mẹ would have made because she saw the restaurant as a fun place for customers. Conversely, Mẹ saw it as an avenue to financial success.

Mẹ's lack of language also resulted in her refusing help in the kitchen. She couldn't have anyone work with her if she couldn't explain what she wanted them to do, and she was picky and uncompromising about how things should be done. All of that led to even more frustration, which she conveyed the only way she knew how: by yelling and storming out of the restaurant.

The main way Mẹ communicated with the world was through her food. When she made something delicious for someone, it made both of them happy. So, another part of the problem was that she felt if she hired another cook, that would diminish her connection with her guests. She didn't know that most restaurants operate with an executive chef who creates the dishes and a support staff that executes them. Mẹ didn't realize that her identity—and her connection with her guests—could still be intact if she wasn't the one making every dish from start to finish.

Not only did that result in Mẹ working harder than she needed to, and becoming even more frustrated, but it was also the reason for Hy Vong's notoriously slow service.

Lastly, Mẹ's view of business was very practical and simple, as it was in Vietnam. She felt that if she worked hard, she should see the money right away. She didn't understand the need to do things that were in the long-term interest of the restaurant but didn't net immediate cash.

For instance, the first time Kathy wanted to do a cooking class and tasting at the South Beach Wine and Food Festival, Mẹ screamed that it was a waste of time and money. She also said if Kathy insisted on participating, Kathy would have to do all of the preparations herself.

That's when I stepped in. I tried to prevent at least some of Mẹ's frustration from landing on Kathy. I explained Kathy's perspective to her in a way that she could understand. She never got upset with me. She would stop yelling and listen. "This is good for you. It will help you get more customers!" I said to her over and over.

Then I called Kathy. I didn't say anything about Mẹ's anger. Instead, I offered suggestions for changes that might help. "Maybe you should at least get them to pay for the ingredients," I said. "Or they can give you a percentage to help cover the costs."

I had spent my whole life acting as the main bridge holding Mẹ and Kathy together. I tried to help both understand what was important to the other. I tried to navigate their strong wills. I tried to play peacekeeper.

On one visit home, Mẹ brought me a household bill and asked, "How do I pay this?" We sat at the dining room table with a blank check. I showed her where to put the dollar amounts, how to write them in English, and how to write the name of the payee. Next, I wrote a numbers cheat sheet on a piece of paper that she could reference when I wasn't there: "1: one, 2: two, 3: three," and so forth up to ten. Then I wrote "100: hundred, 1000: thousand" and gave it to her. I added a kiss on her head. I was so proud of her for trying to read and write English.

Mẹ kept this sheet taped to a wall at home to reference when she needed to write checks. I didn't realize that simple piece of paper would become such an important step in her move toward more independence. I didn't realize that her tension with Kathy had come to a head, and now after years of threatening to break out on her own, she was finally ready to do something about it.

Mac and Cheese

Tung merged this very American dish with her longtime secret weapon—fish sauce. Just a small amount, added while the ground beef cooks, adds big flavor to this pasta-and-meat combination.

SERVES 8 TO 10

1 lb [455 g] elbow macaroni

¼ cup [55 g] unsalted butter

6 medium garlic cloves, roughly chopped

½ medium sweet onion, chopped

1¾ lb [800 g] ground beef

2 tsp fish sauce

½ tsp Accent Flavor Enhancer (optional)

¼ tsp kosher salt

4 cups [455 g] shredded Colby-Jack cheese

Preheat the oven to 350° F [180° C], with a rack in the middle position.

Meanwhile, cook the macaroni according to the package directions. Rinse with cold water and set aside. In a large skillet, melt the butter over medium-high heat, add the garlic, and cook, stirring occasionally, until lightly browned. Add the onion and cook, stirring occasionally, for about 1 minute. Add the ground beef, breaking it up with a wooden spoon or spatula.

Lower the heat to low, stir in the fish sauce, Accent (if using), and salt and cook for about 2 minutes. Raise the heat to medium and cook, stirring occasionally to incorporate the juices, until the beef is cooked through, about 5 minutes more. Off the heat, stir in the reserved macaroni, then transfer the mixture into a 9 by 13 in [23 by 33 cm] pan. Scatter the cheese evenly across the top. Cover the pan tightly with aluminum foil, leaving some space between the top of the macaroni and the foil. Bake until the cheese is melted, 5 to 10 minutes.

CHAPTER 16

Tung Vietnamese Restaurant

Miami, 1997 to 1998

TUNG:

"I'm leaving," I told Kathy. This time, I meant it.

I felt I had worked for twenty years with so little to show for it. This had to change. It wasn't like the times I stormed out of Hy Vong, then returned the next day. Or the time I made Kathy walk home from jail but we still opened the restaurant together the next day. Or one of the many times I got mad, so mad, at Kathy for giving away yet another order of bánh cuốn, the pork-stuffed rice papers that we called pork rolling cakes.

It was bad enough when she gave away something that was easy to make. But the rolling cakes? It had taken me years to perfect my method of soaking and puréeing the rice, then chilling the resulting batter. I had ordered a special cloth-covered steamer from Vietnam in which to turn spoonfuls of that batter into fresh rice papers. I made each rice paper one at a time. I spread the batter onto the hot fabric. I used just the right amount of pressure and timing to ease the soft cooked rice paper off the steamer with a flat bamboo stick. I knew that any sudden move, any change in my timing or my rhythm, would mean that the delicate circle would tear and have to be thrown away.

After I made each paper, I immediately filled it. My filling had also taken years of experimenting to get just right. I found I got the best flavor from a combination of ground pork and Chinese black mushrooms. If I used too much filling, if I rolled the paper too roughly, the cakes would fall apart.

Making enough pork rolling cakes for one dinner service at Hy Vong took hours and hours of standing in one place, repeating the same delicate actions. They were so popular that some customers asked for two or three orders, and we often ran out. Why couldn't Kathy appreciate all of the work and time that went into bánh cuốn? Why didn't she charge more for them, instead of giving so many away for free?

I was so tired of everything about Kathy and Hy Vong. I was so tired of our landlord coming into the restaurant and asking for the rent. I was so tired of not having enough money to put a new roof on the house. I had worked too hard for too long, just working, working—and for what?

I had always assumed that Kathy and I would go our separate ways one day, and I felt that now was the time. It was the fall of 1997, and Phuong Lien was in her last year at Harvard. Now that she was grown up, I felt the independence I needed to open my own restaurant.

I knew I would need some help. Someone had to run the dining room while I cooked—someone who spoke better English than I did. I had been thinking about Carlos, a tall, skinny, dark-haired busboy who had worked at Hy Vong for the past ten years. He was young, seemed honest, and had grown up in America, so he spoke perfect English.

One day before dinner service, Carlos and I were alone in the restaurant. "I want to open a restaurant," I said. "Will you come work with me? You could run the front and order stuff."

He smiled, interested in starting something new. "Sure. When?"

We quickly found a restaurant space for lease 15 miles [24 km] south, in South Dade. The business and all the equipment were for sale. It was twice as big as Hy Vong, and cheap, too. Everything was so dirty—the walls of the kitchen were coated in a thick layer of grease—but I knew I could clean it all up. I loved how open the restaurant felt, and I especially loved the automatic dishwasher and the huge refrigerator that you could walk into. I had never had one of those before. "I know you want to sell fast," I said to the owner. "I will pay you $25,000, and you don't have to clean it."

After the deal was done, I told Kathy that she could come visit the new restaurant, and that we could keep living together. We just couldn't work together.

In December 1997, I opened the doors of Tung Vietnamese Restaurant. I decided to serve the same menu as at Hy Vong, which Kathy was still running. I kept the prices the same, too, figuring I would eventually raise them after more people started coming in. I also decided to serve the same size portions. I was tempted to cut them down, but I was concerned that Hy Vong customers would complain if I did.

There was no reason to shop for food. I just had everything delivered. When the delivery men came, I looked at the cheat sheet that Phuong Lien had made me and wrote the dollar amount on the check. I signed it, then asked each driver to fill in the rest of the information.

I loved paying the bills myself. I loved when new customers told me that the food was good. I especially loved seeing so many of my Hy Vong customers, who came to the kitchen window and told me they were happy for me. "I'm happy, too," I replied.

I knew I had made the right decision when I saw the review in the *Miami Herald* a few months later. The story said my food was "exceptional."

KATHY:

I snipped the *Miami Herald* review out of the paper. I walked over to the front door of Hy Vong and taped it next to the sign I had already posted with the name of Tung's new restaurant and the address. No matter what had happened between us, I only wished her the best. Like Phuong Lien knew that I would always be there if she needed me and that I loved her unconditionally, I hoped that Tung knew that, too.

Then I walked back into the kitchen to start cooking. Now, I was the one spending hours in the Hy Vong kitchen, all by myself, with no one to talk to. I cried as much as I cooked. I knew how to make our food, from years and years of watching and often helping Tung. Still, now I had to do everything myself. I had to start work early in the morning in order to finish all of the shopping and prepping in time. I refused to have food delivered. The quality would never be the same as when I selected it myself.

Tung and I rarely ran into each other at home. On Monday, when our respective restaurants were closed, Tung worked in the garden all day. I got up early and drove to Hy Vong to prepare food for the week.

Monday was my pork-rolling-cake day. I felt pressured to keep serving them. They were the most popular dish at Hy Vong by far. I knew it used to bother Tung when I sometimes gave them away, but I did it because I cared about our customers and was so proud of her creations.

That said, after several Mondays of standing for hours to prepare the labor-intensive cakes, I started to see things from her perspective—and also gained a new appreciation for her dedication and skill. Even after many attempts, I wasn't able to create the delicate morsels that melted in your mouth. I tried using store-bought rice noodles, but they didn't taste the same.

Finally, I took the rolling cakes off the menu. Our customers were such regulars, often coming in once or twice a week, that they could tell the slightest change in the food. It was never an issue when Tung was there; she had a talent for executing the dishes so consistently. Unfortunately, I did not.

One night, a regular poked his head into the kitchen with a sympathetic look on this face. "Kathy," he said gently, "your ribs are a little off." He smiled at me and wrapped me in a hug. I knew he gave me the feedback to help me, but it still hurt that he was leaving unhappy.

I knew things were different in the dining room, too, now that I was no longer out there. My busboys kept things running while I cooked, but I still fretted about whether my customers were being taken care of. And it was no secret that many of them were dining at both Hy Vong and Tung's now, which was a little awkward for all of us. "It's like we are children in the middle of a divorce," said a longtime customer.

+ + +

I'd been on my own at Hy Vong for a few months when I couldn't deny it any longer: I needed Tung's help to run the restaurant. I couldn't do everything myself. But the truth was, I wasn't that good at the business end of things even when Tung was in the kitchen. Maybe it was time to face that reality, too.

What *was* I good at? Taking care of people. Making sure they were happy and didn't need anything. I missed being needed, especially now that I was spending all night in the kitchen alone.

With Phuong Lien away at college, I also missed taking care of a child. I knew from my days in Harlem that I was good with difficult kids. So my ears perked up when a customer told me about an agency that was looking for people to take care of challenging foster children who had experienced violence or abuse. As soon as I heard that, I thought about Grandma Peterson. *That is what I would be good at.* I could help children whom no one else wanted.

I took five hours off each week from Hy Vong to take foster parenting classes at the local foster care agency. At an agency picnic, I got to meet a bunch of kids and laughed and cheered as we played softball and tag. They reminded me of Tung when she first came to live with me. They were getting the short end of the stick. It wasn't their fault that they faced so many challenges. Everyone deserved an opportunity in life, and I knew that I could give those children a chance, just as I had tried to give Tung.

I decided to close Hy Vong sometime in the near future and become a foster parent. It was one of the hardest decisions I had ever made, but I had started to make peace with it by the time Tung and I attended Phuong Lien's graduation from Harvard in the spring of 1998. The weekend felt like old times with just the three of us. Even better, Tung and I were no longer working together, so we had nothing to argue about. We could just laugh and have fun, and focus on our pride for our little girl.

A day after we all flew back to Miami, Tung called me.

"I can't find Carlos, and I am missing $7,500 from the bank. What do I do?" she asked.

I felt terrible for Tung. She was still so naive and trusting. "I will come and help you," I replied.

She didn't want to report Carlos to the police—she didn't believe in revenge. She just wanted to move forward but felt that she couldn't do it without the money, or without Carlos. I put my own plans on hold and helped her close Tung Vietnamese Restaurant. Fortunately, she managed to sell the business for $40,000. Not only was that $15,000 more than her purchase price, but she had already paid off the loan in less than a year.

Her $40,000 in profit was more money—by far—than we had ever earned in one chunk in almost twenty years at Hy Vong!

I had to admit that while Tung still had plenty to learn about people, I had a lot to learn from her when it came to business. I was also very appreciative when she used a chunk of that money to pay for a new roof on our house and new windows that could withstand hurricanes.

With everything that had happened, I began to have doubts about closing Hy Vong and becoming a foster parent. There was one thing that could definitely change my mind, so I took a chance: I asked Tung to come back.

To this day, Tung remembers that she answered only after I promised to pay the electricity and water bills on time. All I heard—and still remember—was the word *yes*. That meant my restaurant and my family were back together again.

Pork Rolling Cakes (Bánh Cuốn)

At Hy Vong, no dish ever came close to selling as well as our pork rolling cakes. It was the most difficult and labor-intensive dish Tung made at the restaurant. She could have simplified it—making thicker rice papers in a pan instead of in a steamer, and topping them with the meat instead of rolling them, for instance—but Tung never believed in compromising ingredients, quality, or taste.

Aside from practice and patience, creating the most delicate rice papers requires a special Vietnamese fabric-covered steamer. Bánh cuốn steamers, as well as fabric-covered rings you can attach to a conventional steamer, are available on Amazon. Tung uses one that measures 10½ in [26.5 cm] in diameter. You also need a long, flat bamboo stick—Tung's measures about 15 in [38 cm] long—which often comes in a set with the fabric-covered steamers. If you don't want to invest in a fabric-covered steamer, Tung doesn't recommend making the rice papers in a skillet, which many people do, because the results are inferior. However, to experience the same wonderful savory rolling cake flavors, it's still well worth preparing the filling and toppings, and serving them over fresh store-bought rice noodles as detailed in the variation below.

Tung generally starts the recipe the night before she wants to serve the rolling cakes, but you can make the rice paper batter and filling up to 2 days in advance. If you choose to use the optional bean sprouts as a topping, scald them first so their crispness doesn't overpower the delicate cakes: Cover them with water in a pot, bring to a boil, then immediately drain and rinse them in cold water.

MAKES ABOUT 10 TWO-CAKE SERVINGS

continued

199

RICE PAPERS

1 cup [200 g] long-grain white rice

½ cup [100 g] short-grain white rice, combined with the long-grain rice, covered with water, and soaked at room temperature for 12 to 24 hours

1 Tbsp cornstarch or tapioca flour

FILLING

2 Tbsp unsalted butter

2 Tbsp chopped garlic

12 oz [340 g] ground pork

4 oz [110 g] ground turkey (not only white meat)

¾ oz [20 g] dried wood ear mushrooms, also known as dried Chinese black fungus, soaked in water at room temperature for 12 to 24 hours, drained, and finely chopped in a food processor

2 tsp fish sauce

¾ tsp turbinado sugar

½ tsp kosher salt

¼ tsp black pepper

¼ tsp Accent Flavor Enhancer (optional)

TOPPINGS

About 8 oz [230 g] bean sprouts, scalded (see headnote; optional)

Leaves from ½ bunch mint, chopped

½ cup [22 g] Fried Shallots (page 28)

4 green onions, sliced

2½ cups [600 ml] Nước Chấm (page 105)

TO MAKE THE RICE PAPERS:

Drain the rice in a fine-mesh strainer, then wash it with cold water twice. (If you don't have a fine-mesh strainer, simply pour off the water and wash the rice in the bowl, changing the water and washing it twice.)

Place the drained rice in a blender and add 1½ cups [360 ml] of water. Blend on high speed until completely liquefied into a soupy consistency, about 4 or 5 minutes. (If the batter starts to thicken, that's a sign that it is starting to overblend; add a little more water, then stop blending.) Transfer the mixture to a large bowl and whisk in the cornstarch. Cover and refrigerate the batter until cold, about 1 hour. The batter will keep, tightly covered, in the refrigerator for up to 2 days.

TO MAKE THE FILLING:

In a large skillet, heat the butter and garlic over medium-high heat until the butter melts. Lower the heat to low and cook, stirring occasionally, until the garlic is golden brown, about 3 minutes.

Add the pork, turkey, ground mushrooms, fish sauce, sugar, salt, pepper, and Accent (if using) and mix well. Cook, stirring constantly to coat the meat with the juices, until the meat is cooked through, 15 to 20 minutes. That will ensure that the meat is moist.

Turn off the heat, spread the filling evenly on the bottom of the skillet, and let cool to room temperature. The filling will keep, in an airtight container, in the refrigerator for up to 2 days. Gently warm to room temperature when you are ready to make the rice papers and assemble the cakes. If the meat is any warmer than room temperature, it may be uncomfortable to roll the cakes with your hands.

TO FINISH THE DISH:

When the batter has chilled and the filling is ready, add enough water to the steamer pot until it hits just below the insert. Bring to a boil over high heat. Meanwhile, wet the fabric and fit it over the steamer insert.

Lightly grease a large plate with some oil and place it next to the stove. Using a ladle, stir the batter well, then scoop 2 Tbsp onto the middle of the fabric and use the bottom of the

continued

ladle to quickly and repeatedly spread it in a circular motion until it forms a 9 in [23 cm] wide circle. Don't worry if it's not perfectly round; this takes a lot of practice. Place the lid on the steamer pot and steam until the batter is cooked through and translucent, 20 to 30 seconds.

Carefully place the long stick underneath the rice paper, lift it, and transfer it to the oiled plate. Scoop a heaping tablespoon of the filling onto the center of the rice paper. Fold two sides over the filling, then roll up the paper from the bottom to form a cylinder.

Carefully transfer the rolling cake with your hands to a serving platter or plate. Repeat with the remaining batter and filling, stirring the batter before each scoop and greasing the plate again, as needed. Stir the filling several times throughout the process to make sure the juices are distributed evenly.

Top the rolling cakes with the bean sprouts (if using), mint, fried shallots, and green onions. Drizzle with the nước chấm (¼ cup [60 ml] per serving of two rolling cakes) or serve the sauce on the side. Serve the cakes as they are ready, if you like.

VARIATION:

To make Pork Rolling Cake–Style Rice Noodles, for each serving use 6 oz [170 g] fresh rice noodles (available at Asian grocery stores). Cut the noodles into 2 in [5 cm] lengths and microwave, covered, until warm. Top with about ½ cup [55 g] hot or warm pork rolling cake filling, then top with some bean sprouts, mint, fried shallots, green onions, and about ¼ cup [60 ml] nước chấm. The amount of filling and toppings in the main recipe are enough to make about 7 servings of this noodle variation.

CHAPTER 17

Appreciation

Miami, 1998 to 2006

TUNG:

I wasn't sure if I could trust anyone again. I felt so betrayed by Carlos's disappearance and the missing money. I had been so good to him. How could he have treated me like this? I could have kept my own restaurant going for years and years. Now I was back at Hy Vong, and I felt defeated.

I didn't want to fight with Kathy, and she seemed to feel the same way. She seemed to appreciate me more. She was calmer, quieter. While I was gone, she had hired Jay, a quiet young guy from Central America, to help her with food preparation. Jay didn't seem to know how to do anything.

After we met, I gave him 5 pounds [2.3 kg] of shrimp to clean. I checked back an hour later to find a pile of ruined shrimp and Jay looking in confusion at his knife. I remembered my early days working at the Rusty Pelican when I was pregnant; I had no idea how to clean shrimp the way my boss wanted it done.

I took the knife from Jay. "Pinch the tail," I said. "Remove the shell fast. Peel with your fingers from the bottom up." I made him do everything right next to me so I could watch. Jay didn't react like so many of the other people that Kathy had tried to hire over the years. He didn't talk more than he worked. He said almost nothing. He just nodded and tried again. When I told him he was still doing it wrong, he nodded and tried again. I thought about getting rid of him, but he kept coming back.

Six weeks later, he could clean shrimp as well as I could. I moved him on to stock. I showed him how many bones needed to be in the pot with the water. After a few weeks, I let Jay make his own stock from start to finish. It was too thin, but I knew why, because by then I knew more about Jay.

Like me, he had grown up in the countryside. He barely spoke English, and his eyes carried the same lonely, hollow look that I recognized from looking in the mirror after I had first arrived in Miami. He worked as hard as I did. He hadn't put enough bones in the stock because he was used to being poor and hungry. He wanted the bones to last longer. I understood that feeling.

I kept checking his pot during every new attempt, letting him taste the finished stock so that he understood the difference between a good and bad one. Eventually, he got it—and everything else I taught him. Jay was the first person I could trust, really trust, to make my food.

It was just in time. Hy Vong was now rated in the Miami Zagat guide, the little red book of restaurant reviews that everyone in the city seemed to have. We were starting to show up in travel guidebooks, too. We were busier than ever and we had to find a way to serve people faster. I found that if I trusted Jay, we could.

LYN:

After I graduated from Harvard, I started working long hours in investment banking in Manhattan. I always ordered out for lunch, and usually dinner, too. I lived on the basic American fare I had always favored: salads, steak, and pasta.

Whenever I went to Miami to visit, Mẹ would send me off with containers of homemade food that was easy to warm up. Those dishes spared me from yet another monotonous round of takeout, so I came to regard them with new appreciation. For the first time, I didn't just eat Mẹ's tender beef with fresh rice noodles: I really savored the dish. Its shallot and mint garnish added freshness and complexity that I never found in my typical meals.

Most often, Mẹ made me spicy ribs, one of her most rustic dishes. She slowly braised pork spareribs that she had cleaved into small, bite-off-the-bone pieces, in her signature stock with fish sauce and a hefty pinch of bird's-eye chiles. As I dug into the dish, I noticed the moistness of the ribs, the richness of the broth. I couldn't get enough.

Similar to my experience seeking out those Vietnamese restaurants near Harvard, I began to crave those complex and fiery scents and flavors that I had spent my childhood scorning. I also realized that Mẹ's food was leagues above everything I was eating in New York—even at the fanciest business dinners.

A light bulb went off in my head. I finally understood why Hy Vong's customers spent so much time waiting for a table and dealt with the inconvenience of stepping outside to use the restroom.

After I earned an MBA at Cornell University in 2005, I started to wonder if there were ways to grow Hy Vong, without all the intensely physical work and time involved in running a restaurant.

For a few years, the three of us joined forces on a prepared foods business, which we managed to run in addition to the restaurant. Mẹ's pork rolling cakes, phở, curried chicken and sweet potatoes, and other signature dishes were sold at eight Miami-area gourmet grocery stores. Often, when we were stocking the shelves, we would bump into Hy Vong customers who were so thankful to have Mẹ's cooking without the long waits for a table. And every day the stores would sell out, and customers would ask the managers for more.

During the time I worked directly with Mẹ and Kathy, I got a closer look into their relationship. From the outside, they looked like a mess. The new sense of calm after they reunited at Hy Vong did not last long. They still fought like cats and dogs. Mẹ yelled and screamed, calling Kathy "crazy monkey." Kathy paced and forgot what she had done a few seconds earlier. Her hair began to stick out in every direction, and in a frazzled tone, she kept asking Mẹ questions that my mother refused to answer.

Any stranger watching would wonder how these two women could work together for a few hours, never mind decades. But that was just their way.

"You know," Kathy told me at one point, "We do actually know how to work together." Mẹ's yelling was just part of Kathy's normal day, and Kathy's frazzled nature was just part of Mẹ's normal day. More important, both are easily eclipsed by the sounds of their satisfied customers happily slurping the last drops from their bowls.

When it comes to the success of Hy Vong, I give Kathy much more credit than Mẹ does. Yes, I thought that Kathy never understood how to manage money. She was not always responsible about paying the bills, but they eventually got paid. She always bought excellent-quality food, even if she didn't do it in the most efficient manner. And most important, Kathy always kept pushing the restaurant forward and built an incredible family of extremely loyal customers. Even when things got rough, she refused to quit, as long as Mẹ would go along for the ride.

Why has their friendship endured for so many years, despite so many differences in culture and personality? Their values are the same. They share a firm sense of right and wrong. They take care of others who need help, even when doing so makes their own lives harder. They both always stand on their own two feet, proudly defining and making their own success.

Beneath all of their bluster lies a strong trust in each other. Kathy continued to love and believe in Mẹ even though she was often not very nice to her. Mẹ got angry and upset on almost a nightly basis and occasionally walked out of Hy Vong, but she always returned because she felt something larger was at stake.

How Mẹ benefited from Kathy is obvious. But Kathy also benefited from having Mẹ in her life, and I understand better than most people why she stuck with my mother through all of those fights and all of those years. Mẹ provided Kathy with a fundamental stability. She showed Kathy that there was a more fulfilling path than hopping around between short-term jobs and different cities and living alone. She happily helped make a home, cooking, cleaning, and gardening—all things Kathy didn't want to do.

Kathy and Mẹ might have been born in different countries, with different cultures, languages, and expectations, but they worked through all of their differences to build something very powerful together. They showed me that we are all bigger than our individual selves, and that our lives can celebrate the best parts of each individual, while forging the path that is best for each of us.

I never dwelled much on my ethnic background or culture when I was growing up. Mẹ didn't act like the other Vietnamese women I met who were chatty and gossipy and constantly comparing who was doing what. I never related to the emphasis on material wealth that I saw when we visited Vietnam, nor to the women's subservience to men.

Perhaps that's because Mẹ and Kathy didn't either. Unlike other parents who hope their daughter will get married, they always worried that a man would hold me down and assume a patriarchal role. They wanted me to dream big and go after my ambitions. They always supported that my career came first, and they never asked me to move back to Miami or take over the restaurant.

They also supported me when I changed my name. After I spent a few years in the corporate world, I decided to stop going by Phuong Lien and start calling myself Lyn. I was tired of explaining the pronunciation of my name in the largely Caucasian, all-male business meetings I regularly attended. I figured that "Lyn" was close enough to the second half of my name. Kathy and Tung accepted this practical reasoning, though they continue to call me Phuong Lien or Phuongy at home.

I embrace the strong sense of family obligation that I see in Vietnamese culture. However, I'm not sure whether I inherited that from Mẹ or from Kathy, or from both of them. Mẹ, of course, always made her parents, brothers, and sister her top priority, after me. But Kathy, too, stayed close with her family and nursed my grandmother—her mother—around the clock when she grew sick and finally passed away in 2001.

Mẹ never told me the real story about my birth father until we began to work on this book. Even then, I didn't learn about it from her: I was first told by our writer, Elisa Ung, who had been filled in by Kathy. I suppose I should have been more shocked, but I wasn't. It just fell in a long line of painful details that our work on the book revealed about Mẹ's life.

Most of Kathy and Mẹ's influence on me has little to do with their cultural backgrounds and everything to do with them as individuals. They are hard-working, hard-headed, determined, often irrational women who defy boundaries. So am I.

During my investment banking and early career years, I financed technology companies, learning and understanding how software could change the way people approached business problems. I used this knowledge to create something that also defied boundaries and helped transform how business leaders apply artificial intelligence to optimize risk and profit. In 2008 I built Liquid Analytics, which now has offices in the United States and Canada, and a list of global clients. I continually rely on my roots, whether that involves creating delightful novel experiences from scratch, delivering uncompromising quality, or navigating personalities.

Mẹ and Kathy shaped my entrepreneurial DNA. They showed me how to believe that there is nothing I can't do—from installing an air-conditioning line to building a company. They showed me there are no limits to my life. And that family is whom you choose.

Spicy Ribs (Thịt Sườn)

The pungent punch behind this dish comes from bird's-eye chiles—a hot, fruity variety commonly used in Vietnamese, Thai, and other Southeast Asian cuisines. The powdered version is available online or at Asian grocery stores, but you can also make your own by grinding whole dried bird's-eyes in a food processor, clean coffee grinder, or mortar and pestle. It takes about 14 chiles to yield the amount of powder needed in this recipe.

SERVES 4 TO 6

¼ cup [60 ml] fish sauce

2 Tbsp lime juice

1 Tbsp sugar

3 lb [1.4 kg] pork spareribs, trimmed of excess fat, separated, and cleaved into 2 in [5 cm] pieces by a butcher

1 small sweet onion, chopped

1 Tbsp dried bird's-eye chile powder

2½ cups [600 ml] Hy Vong Stock (page 66), hot or warm

4 to 6 cups [480 to 720 g] cooked jasmine rice, for serving

3 green onions, sliced, for garnish

In a large pot, add the fish sauce, 1 Tbsp [5 ml] of the lime juice, and the sugar and mix well. Add the ribs, sweet onion, and chile powder and mix well.

Cover the pot and cook over medium heat for about 10 minutes. Stir, cover again, and cook for 15 minutes more. Stir, add the stock, and bring to a boil over high heat. Lower the heat and simmer, uncovered, until the ribs are tender, about 10 minutes. Stir in the remaining 1 Tbsp of lime juice. Serve with rice and top with the green onions.

CHAPTER 18

American

Miami and Vietnam, 2004 to 2015

TUNG:

One day in 2004, my mother called to tell me that she was not feeling well. I sent my brothers money to take her to a hospital. A few days later, my brother Kiem called to tell me that my mother had died at home. They had never taken her to get medical care. She was eighty-four years old.

I cried, mourning not just my mother, but also her chance to live an even longer life. I sent more money—about $400—for my mother's headstone. I wanted it to be made of shiny white marble, not the cheap dark hard rock from the mountainside that most of the other peasants used. She would be buried near Bà Nội and my father in the village cemetery.

Kathy and I were busy with the restaurant and could not get back to Vietnam in time for my mother's funeral, but we decided that once the headstone was finished, we would go back to see it.

We also wanted to see the village's new Buddhist temple, which I had sent money to help build.

I could have sent all the money in the world, and it would never have been enough for everything my family and Điện Bàn needed. Like most of the villagers, my siblings were paid very little for their hours and hours of labor. They worked so hard, yet they still had trouble paying the bills. They were angry and frustrated, and their anger and frustration came to a head during my visit with them to our mother's grave in 2005.

We visited the village Buddhist temple to burn incense and fake money, as we usually did when honoring the dead. We talked and ate. I had no idea what was brewing, but the trouble started right after Kathy left the gathering with one of my nephews, who was taking her back to the hotel.

I was standing talking to a relative outside the temple when my brother Nhut suddenly turned on me. "You cheated me out of your money," he screamed. Then he and Kiem pushed and shoved me, and yanked my purse out of my hand. Nhut grabbed my arm and dragged me outside. "I am going to beat you up!" he continued. "I should have gotten more money!"

Thankfully, Kathy was still close enough to see the ruckus and told my nephew to turn his motorcycle around. "Get away from her!" she yelled at Nhut and Kiem as she ran toward us. Kathy screamed for me to get on my niece's motorcycle, and the four of us rode back to the hotel. Most of my family later joined us, cursing Nhut and Kiem.

My heart was broken. I had worked so hard to try to help everyone, giving them everything I could, and they were so ungrateful.

I left Điện Bàn right after that and never returned. I had visited all of those times because I missed my family and my community. Now, with my mother gone, things were different. Too many people, including some of my siblings, valued me only as a source of money. I no longer belonged in that family or community.

Kathy and I continued to send money specifically for two of my nephews' educations, but now I needed to focus my attention and money on my family in America—Phuong Lien, Kathy, and our customers. The United States was now my home. It had embraced me. It had welcomed me. It had helped me rise higher than I had ever dreamed of. This was where I belonged.

+ + +

I had arrived a scared refugee, afraid of the spark from Kathy's gas stove, scared to sit down at a table of people who had left more wealth in Vietnam than I could even imagine. Now America was home, and I had plenty to be proud of. Starting in the 1990s, Hy Vong was highly rated in Zagat and Miami tourism guidebooks. Our home was beautiful, too, thanks to one of our customers, Candy, who was an architect. He offered to design and manage our renovations at such a discount that we got way more than we could have afforded otherwise.

Now we had custom-made cabinets, gleaming new tile, double ovens . . . Once the work was done, I said to Kathy, "Let's invite Bà Hien and her daughter over for dinner." I was ready to settle a three-decades-old score.

I had met Bà Hien at the immigration office when I got my green card in 1979. Kathy had cautioned me not to lie to the immigration agent about my family situation. So when it was my turn at the counter, I said in English, as clearly as I could, "I am not married. I have a daughter." I was ashamed to say those words and could hardly pronounce them.

The agent looked confused. "What?" he said.

I said it again. "I am not married. I have a daughter." He just kept giving me the same look.

He then looked behind me and called to someone, "Can you help translate for me?"

I turned around and saw a well-dressed family. The woman, Bà Hien, greeted me, and I immediately knew from her accent that she was from Hanoi. My mother's words of warning sounded in my head as she and her family glared at me. I could barely compose myself to tell them in my heavy country accent that I was single and had a daughter. They responded by calling me "con," or child, instead of what they would have called me if they considered me an equal: "chị," or sister.

After finishing with the agent, I left the office in tears and humiliation. Kathy filed a complaint, and my green card arrived in the mail quickly.

A year later, after we had opened Hy Vong, Kathy and I were shopping at an Asian wholesale restaurant supplier when I saw the same family. I went up to them and said hello. "How do you know this place?" Bà Hien asked me.

"Kathy brought me here," I said. "She is the American woman I live with. We own a restaurant, Hy Vong."

It turned out that Bà Hien and her husband owned a nearby Asian grocery store. I began to shop there and occasionally spoke to them. On the surface, they said things that were friendly. But they often added a snide comment or a subtle insult to remind me of my position in Vietnamese society. To be respected and be able to socialize with her on an equal level, I needed more than I had. The restaurant wasn't enough. My daughter doing well in school got me closer. I resigned myself to the fact that we would never be friends. It's not that I wanted her as a friend; I just didn't want the reason to be because I was viewed as inferior.

Fast-forward thirty years. Everyone knew Hy Vong. My daughter had gone to Harvard. I had a nice house and bank account. Now I felt that I was equal to Bà Hien. I could socialize with her on her level. And I would do this by inviting her over to our house.

For the first time in years, I purchased a new dress. I made sure that my garden was pruned and in full bloom. I prepared a Vietnamese feast, foods that I imagined wealthier people would have been impressed with in Vietnam: watercress salad, shrimp pâté on sugarcane, barbecue pork with vermicelli, flan for dessert.

I decided to add kimchi to the menu, too. I had been experimenting with it at Hy Vong because our customers had been asking for spicy dishes. My kimchi had all the flavors that I remembered from the tins that dropped from above when I was a child. I knew that it was not Vietnamese, but I thought that Bà Hien and her husband and daughter might enjoy it as much as our customers seemed to. It was also my way of incorporating my country roots into the fancy dinner.

When the family arrived, I showed them our new bathrooms and the new kitchen. I made sure they knew that the house had at least tripled in value from the time that we bought it. I told them about Hy Vong's Zagat rating, and that we were preparing to renovate the restaurant so that it was as beautiful as our home.

For the first time, they looked at me with respect. They said that my food was delicious and my home was beautiful. They called me "chị."

A few months later, Bà Hien asked us over to their house. My heart stopped when I learned of the invitation. Kathy exclaimed, "It has only taken us thirty years!"

KATHY:

We had a great time at Bà Hien's house, although I couldn't help but notice the bathroom tile was nowhere near as nice as ours.

I have rarely been as proud of Tung as I was of her relationship with Bà Hien. Tung had truly evolved into an American. Yes, she could socialize with wealthy Vietnamese people on their level because she *was* at their level, and always had been! She no longer reverted to being submissive when she met richer Vietnamese people. Now she could dream big—and she was!

After we finished renovating our house, I knew Tung wanted to make the restaurant just as beautiful. Honestly, I didn't care if we ever renovated Hy Vong. We were already a success in my book. For years, customers had teased me about how our food was worth going outside for to use the bathroom. Still, I did want them to be more comfortable, and I wanted Tung to have her dream kitchen there, too. Hy Vong had been such a hole in the wall for so long, even though it had gotten bigger when we took over the space next door in the late 1980s. What would be the harm in updating it?

As it turned out, the harm was the cost. Even with the generous discounts Candy secured for us, the project quickly became more expensive than we expected, and the bills kept mounting. I ran up credit card debt. I almost depleted the Lutheran Trivent retirement account that my mother had set up for me when we opened the restaurant back in 1980.

I thought we might have to stop the work. As I sat at the dining room table one day wondering what to do, Tung emerged from her bedroom with a big box of coins and bills that she kept hidden in her closet. She deposited it all on the table, with lots of clanking.

All I could do was laugh and laugh. I had no idea this money even existed. I called Phuongy and exclaimed, "Do you know what your mother just did?" When we counted it, we found that, once again, Tung had saved thousands of dollars from spare change.

That money put us over the finish line. We were able to expand our kitchen and increase our seating area. We unveiled a striking bamboo bar with custom wood countertops, where people could congregate as they waited for a table. Colorful hand-painted murals covered one wall. Best of all, we now had two restrooms right in the restaurant.

"We finally have indoor plumbing!" I announced to customers as they walked into Hy Vong on the day we reopened. "Kathy, it looks beautiful," they said, over and over, hugging me between all the oohs and aahs.

I passed out small bowls of kimchi to start the meal. The humble cabbage had been a surprise hit—I was shocked by how much everyone loved it, as it was so spicy. The bowls were empty a few minutes later, despite my advice to save some to enjoy with the meal.

I could see Tung in the kitchen window, cooking and occa-sionally smiling at a customer telling her how beautiful everything was. She had learned to make this kimchi when she was a child, using a tin that fell from the sky and a cabbage that she had never seen before. Now she presided over her own stunning kitchen and was known as one of the best chefs in Miami.

In some ways, this was even better than my wildest dreams.

Kimchi

Tung uses fresh bird's-eye chiles and ginger to put her own
mark on the traditional Korean fermented cabbage side dish.
This recipe is very close to the one she developed as a child
in Vietnam. The heat of this kimchi became famous among
Hy Vong customers.

MAKES ABOUT 5 CUPS [795 G]

5 oz [140 g] ginger (about a 6 in [15 cm] piece),
peeled and cut into ¼ in [6 mm] thick slices

10 medium garlic cloves

5 fresh bird's-eye chiles, tops removed

1 head (about 2 lb [910 g]) napa cabbage

6 green onions, white parts halved lengthwise,
whites and greens cut into 1 in [2.5 cm] pieces

1 Tbsp kosher salt

In the bowl of a food processor, process the ginger, garlic, and
chiles until minced, stopping short of making a paste. Add
½ cup [120 ml] of water and mix with a spoon. Set aside.

Halve the cabbage lengthwise, then cut each half into strips
about 2 by ½ in [5 cm by 12 mm] long by alternately slicing
diagonally for a few cuts, then slicing diagonally the other way
for another few cuts. Rinse and drain the cabbage.

In a large bowl, combine the cabbage and green onions.
Sprinkle with the salt and thoroughly mix with a spoon or
your hands (use gloves if you prefer). Spread the reserved
ginger mixture over the cabbage mixture. Use a spoon or your
hands to pat it into the cabbage mixture. Cover and let sit in
the warmest part of your home, or outdoors if the temperature
is about 70°F [21°C], for 12 to 14 hours.

Thoroughly mix with a spoon or your hands (use gloves if
you prefer), scoop into one large glass jar or several smaller
ones, and refrigerate. The kimchi will continue to ferment and
will be ready to eat in 3 days. It can keep in the refrigerator for
up to 1 month.

Epilogue

Miami, 2015 to 2020

KATHY:

In 2015, we celebrated being ranked Zagat's #11 restaurant in all of Miami. But later that year, we ran into a major issue with a lease renewal we couldn't afford and realized we would have to close Hy Vong. We made that decision on a Thursday in October and served our last dinner the next day. All of our staff helped us clean out the restaurant. We laughed and reminisced about our thirty-five years in business.

I tried to find another spot so we could reopen, but everything was too expensive or would need major renovations we couldn't afford. We did a number of catering jobs. Then we truly found our groove when we launched a series of pop-up dinners, many of them at a nearby church. That gave us a setting in which we could serve a lot of people at once and watch our customers interact with each other. We could re-create the dinner party–like atmosphere that they always told us they loved.

Our pop-ups, which we continue to this day based on what space is available, are some of the most fun we've ever had. My favorite part is watching Tung socialize. She didn't always have time to really do that at the restaurant, and for years she was too insecure about her language skills. Now in her seventies, like I am, she jumps right into the crowd. A few times I've gone to the kitchen to look for her, only to realize that she was making the rounds of customers without me!

These events crystallize the most special part of Hy Vong: a community of people who supported each other and our family. A community of people who accepted Tung and me for who we were, rather than judging us for who they thought we should be. A community that got to know us as people, not just as people serving them food. A community that helped us thrive because they fixed broken doors and plumbing, gave us advice and loans, and pitched in when our staff called in sick or we needed anything else.

In 1989, Rafael Navarro wrote in the *Miami New Times*: "Hy Vong is a bite-size marvel of a place. It's got food that aims high, and reaches its destination. More important, it's got soul, a conscience—humanity."

That right there was my business plan.

When Tung moved into my house all those years ago, I could have regarded her as a woman from Vietnam who cooked well. I could have eaten her food and sent her on her way. I could have listened to my friend Thao, and believed that Tung would never understand anything I said.

Instead, I chose to get to know Tung as a person, and in doing so, I gained much more than I gave to her. I gained a unique picture of cultural assimilation. I got to travel to Vietnam. I got to learn about farmers, food, music, stories, language, and culture. I learned to be open and not assume things about other people. I learned that it was possible to have stability and family roots in a way that made sense to me, even if it seemed unorthodox to others.

Tung and I seemed like we had nothing in common, and certainly we struggled through our differences. Tung and I fought with each other plenty, but that fighting turned into embracing each other. In the end, we shared enough common values that we could create a life together, and join forces to raise Phuong Lien the best we knew how. Just look at our daughter now!

People who simply eat the food of refugees and immigrants, but don't get to know them as people, miss a golden opportunity. Refugees are here because they have no choice. They also bring enormous gifts and talents, as Tung did. They just need an opportunity.

I hope our story inspires others to understand that people from different backgrounds can find common ground if we just listen to each other. We can all be bigger than our individual selves. We all have tremendous power to change the lives of others and help the world become more mixed and accepting.

That applies as much to people in the countryside of Vietnam—who have been raised to believe they are second-class citizens—as it does to those of us living comfortable lives in America. Everyone can get to know people who are different than they are. Everyone can help where they see a need. We all have stories to tell, and the best thing we can do for ourselves and the world is to listen to each other.

TUNG:

Now that my story has been told, I feel free. My head is clear. For years, it was easiest for me to try to forget so many events in my life. Remembering those stories and all of their painful details has opened new wounds, but it has closed many, too.

I never realized that my story might be interesting to people. I never thought my story might even inspire others. For most of my life, I just wanted to belong. Cooking was how I belonged. I am so proud to have cooked food that made so many different types of people happy. In Vietnam, I could never gain the respect of wealthy people. In America, my background and my status didn't matter, except to other Vietnamese. American doctors, lawyers, celebrities, teachers, parents, and children all ate my food. They helped me, praised me, and gave me the confidence to share more about my life.

The first time I saw people at a dinner stand up and clap for me, I was overwhelmed. All I could do is cry and think, *They stood up for me? Someone from the country? Someone who never finished elementary school?*

I hope our story helps others understand that everyone can belong, even if they grew up poor, like me, or just different, like Kathy. What matters is how hard people work, what they make of themselves, and how they help others grow, too.

Most of all, I am grateful to Kathy for our friendship and for the life we built together. I am grateful for the opportunities she gave me, and the opportunities she gave my daughter—all of which we never could have had in Vietnam. She opened doors, supported me, and believed in me. She is now more like family to me than my family in Vietnam. She has even learned to listen to me! Kathy may drive me crazy, but she has a good heart. A beautiful heart. That is what I treasure most.

Acknowledgments

Writing our first book has been an adventure! It was also an emotional roller coaster and often a test of patience, but through the many funny and heated moments, *Mango and Peppercorns* grew page by page.

The idea for the book was inadvertently born several years earlier at a coffee shop in Coconut Grove, Florida. Lyn was sitting with our friend Lee Schrager, founder of the South Beach Wine and Food Festival, when he suddenly announced, "You should write a book." Lee's belief in us, and his introductions within the publishing world, gave us the conviction to begin this journey.

No book is created without an incredible team. *Mango and Peppercorns*'s team started with Alison Fargis, our agent. Her enthusiasm, advice, and constant championing has guided us every step of the way. Thank you for playing referee with multiple strong-willed authors. Thank you for taking a chance on us. We could not have done this without you.

Elisa Ung has been our behind-the-scenes heroine, who interviewed us, wrote our stories, and tested our recipes. "I don't think Tung wants to talk to me anymore" were words she often repeated. After an especially intense interview. After questioning Tung about a recipe for the third time. After requesting even more personal details. She patiently listened to our often-random stories. She made connections that we'd never even thought of. She probed deeper into our memories and histories than any of us expected. None of it was easy, but the book is much richer and more authentic because of it. We are honored to have worked with someone with as much creativity and integrity as Elisa.

Short deadlines, multiple voices and opinions, complex recipes, and personal photographs. Our editor, Kathy Brennan, read and edited multiple versions of our memoir. She challenged the recipes to ensure their authenticity and accessibility. Thank you, Kathy, for your insightful and fresh perspective.

Mango and Peppercorns bridges two cultures and two languages. Nhi Huynh, thank you for helping with our cultural and translation questions.

Thank you to Dan Gerstein and Michael Signorelli of Gotham Ghostwriters for matching us with Elisa; Raquel Pelzel for referring us to Alison; Marc Schwarz for providing valuable early editorial feedback; Camaren Subhiyah, who had the vision to turn our cookbook proposal into a memoir; and especially to our talented book designer, Vanessa Dina; diligent copyeditor Emily Wolman, and proofreader Mikayla Butchart; and the entire editorial team at Chronicle, led by Sarah Billingsley and Cristina Garces, who have all helped turn our words and photos into a beautiful publication. And thank you to Joyce Lin and Cynthia Shannon, Chronicle's publicity and marketing managers, respectively, for your dedication in shepherding the book into the world.

We have fed a lot of people over four decades, and our story is not complete without our customers. You waited outside for hours to get a seat. You walked through the rain to go to the bathroom. After we closed, you stopped us in the middle of the street to tell us you missed our food. We have celebrated first dates, anniversaries, children's birthdays, and graduations with you, and we miss those weekly visits where we knew your order before you said it. You are our Hy Vong family, and for that we are grateful.

We want to give special thanks to our long-time customers and friends Mark Riedmiller, Debra Lundy, Samuel Blum, and Carl Sugarman, who shared their stories for the book. Also, Susan Wittenberg and Carol Stein, who fell so in love with the Hy Vong story that they filmed a soulful mini documentary about it. (It is currently on YouTube, if you are interested in watching it.) We are also indebted to Mitch Kaplan and Mike Kernish for their publishing industry insight and enthusiastic support over the years.

And last, but not least, thank you to Michelle Bernstein. Sometimes, one of your customers becomes a friend and an international celebrity chef. We are honored that Michelle, a trailblazer in the food industry who first dined at our restaurant when she was just twelve years old, wrote the foreword for *Mango and Peppercorns*.

We would be remiss not to mention that Hy Vong would not have survived those early years without the generous media coverage it was so fortunate to receive from our local newspapers, the *Miami Herald* and *New Times*. Thank you to Margarita Fichtner, Lydia Martin, Geoffrey Tomb, Joan Fleischman, and Rafael Navarro for discovering our hidden gem and highlighting the hope, stories, and passion behind the food.